D0875174

"John Arroyo is a paradox. He has every reason to be angry and filled with revenge, depression, and regret because of his being attacked on Fort Hood. Yet, as his book Attacked at Home unravels the details of an active shooter, you will see the unraveling of God's amazing grace in the face of complete hopelessness. Bleeding out and dazed, a Voice, John would become familiar with in years to follow, audibly commanded this young Green Beret to "Get up" when his world was falling down around him. Like a good soldier, he obeyed his newfound Commander and Chief, the King of Kings, and today he still stands, unflinchingly, challenging a young generation to stand up with him for truth and righteousness."

—Dave Roever, Minister, Motivational Speaker, Author, President of Roever Foundation.

"This book is a journey into the guts of gang life in teen years through the inspiring heart of heroism as a Green Beret to a destiny of dedicated service to all mankind. This story of John Arroyo is an uncommon place yet real-life movie material that is a must-read. The realism that pours out of this book flows with the gentleness that undergirds the harshness that Arroyo has experienced and yet gushes with the passion needed to flood the pages with direction, purpose, and meaning. As an educator who stays connected with elementary school campuses to institutions that offer terminal degrees, I highly recommend this book to students of high school and college to gain insight into human life, history, contemporary literature and the life of a man—a man who has been poured out and is willing to be poured out for the sake of people, especially future generations. "Attacked at Home: A Green Beret's Survival Story of the Ft. Hood Shooting" is a journey worth sharing, a life worth recording, and a read that should not be passed up by anyone who cares about life in general or life in America, especially as it relates to young men and women."

**—Dr. Sheba K. George, Superintendent & Founder,
Newman International Academy**

"In a very personal, human interest narrative, John Arroyo sets forth a very readable life story of an individual who grew up in poverty, surrounded by street gangs, to complete a successful career as a U.S. Army Green Beret and later civilian, continuing in a lifetime of service. This success was shaped by a faith instilled early on within his life by a loving grandmother. Equally important is Arroyo's inclusion of his wife's story, as she lived through the challenges and opportunities presented in their life together. This book is a must-read."

**—Dr. Tom Seals, Professor of Biblical Practice
& Chaplain to Veterans, Lipscomb University,
Author of *God's Word for Warriors***

"A powerful testimony of the overcomer's life. John Arroyo's improbable rise from urban gangs to U.S. Army warrior-leadership to mass-shooting survivor to gospel preacher is a classic, faith-stirring epic. Even more remarkable to me was John's ability to accept all life threw at him - successes and failures; triumphs and tragedies - with a trusting, child-like faith in the goodness and possibilities of God. You must read Attacked at Home: A Green Beret's Survival Story of the Ft. Hood Shooting."

**—Tim Moynihan, Pastor, Former U.S. Army Ranger,
Author of *Prodigal Avenger***

"If you want to appreciate what God can do in the life of a person serving in the military, then this book is a must-read. God takes John as he is and walks alongside him as he experiences the near-fatal betrayal by a fellow soldier."

—Colonel Kenneth Sorenson,
(Chaplain) U.S. Army, Active Duty

Therefore take up the whole armor of God,
that you may be able to withstand the evil day,
and having done all, to stand.

—Ephesians 6:13 (NKJV)

DEADLY ENCOUNTER

S tanding by the front of my vehicle, I unexpectedly heard gunfire and instinctively ducked, thinking, *"All of the Taliban and Al Qaeda fighters have been cleared from the base, and ISIS is nowhere near us, so who could be shooting?"* Then I remembered that I was at Fort Hood, Texas, and no longer in Afghanistan or Iraq. It was April 2, 2014.

I noticed an enlisted soldier sitting in a parked car fifteen feet away. I assumed he was trying to determine from which direction the gunshots were coming. Suddenly he raised a .45 caliber Smith & Wesson M&P pistol and fired it point-blank into my face. The bullet tore through my left jugular vein, shattered my voice box, entered my right shoulder, and lodged in my upper arm socket. With my left hand, I quickly grabbed my throat wound and squeezed hard to stop the flow of blood. My right arm was paralyzed and dangled limply by my side.

The moment I was shot, I froze in disbelief. I wasn't sure what had just happened, I remember thinking, *"Am I shot?"* I didn't feel any pain, but the impact felt as if I was hit in the chest with a baseball bat. However, instantly, my worst fears were confirmed when I saw massive amounts of bright red blood flowing through my fingers and down my chest. My first reaction was to get away. I stumbled back to my car and collapsed on the ground. Thoughts began running through my mind, *"Is this it? After all of my combat tours in the Middle East, am I now dying? What will happen to my wife, Angel, and the kids? I don't think Angel can take any more loss after both of her parents have recently died."* All of a sudden, I heard a voice tell me, **"Get up! Get up, or your wife will die!"** The voice didn't come from someone outside. With no urgency in its tone, it came from deep within me and was clear and sharp.

Slowly staggering upright, I stood and tried to cover my throat with my right hand, but realized my right arm wouldn't move at all. I thought, *"Maybe it was broken when I fell down on the parking lot pavement."* As I explain the events now, it might appear that I was taking my time, but my actions were happening in just seconds, not minutes. At that point, there was no one around me, and I knew I needed help fast. I began staggering toward my unit, hoping I would make it there before I passed out.

As I approached the front door of the First Medical Brigade headquarters, I saw a soldier walking toward me. I tried yelling for his help. But nothing came out of my mouth except massive amounts of blood. As the individual and I drew closer to each other on the wide sidewalk, something warned me about his demeanor, and I thought, *"He's walking very calmly but looking around frantically."* Then I realized it was the shooter! Ten feet directly in front of me, he stopped, looked about anxiously, not even acknowledging that I was standing there, turned, walked into the brigade headquarters, and began killing people.

ACKNOWLEDGMENTS:
Design Services by Melinda Martin—Martin Publishing Services
Scriptural Research by Peggy S. Corvin, BA, Master's Degree in Theology.

PUBLISHING INFORMATION:
ICB - Scripture is taken from the International Children's Bible®. Copyright © 1986, 1988, 1999 by Thomas Nelson All rights reserved.
NLT—New Living Translation, copyright © 1996, 2004, 2007 by Tyndale House Foundation. All rights reserved.
NKJV– Scripture is taken from the New King James Version®. Copyright © 1982 by Thomas Nelson. All rights reserved.
NIV—Scripture quotations marked (NIV) are taken from the Holy Bible, New International Version®, and NIV®. Copyright © 1973, 1978, 1984, 2011 by Biblica, Inc. ™ Used by permission of Zondervan. All rights reserved worldwide. The "NIV" and "New International Version" are trademarks registered in the United States Patent and Trademark Office by Biblica, Inc. ™

ISBN: Paperback   978-1-7327625-4-1
        Hardback   978-1-7327625-5-8
        eBook   978-1-7327625-6-5

PUBLISHED BY: Southwestern Legacy Press, LLC
                 P.O. Box 1231
                 Gallatin, TN 37066

LIBRARY CATALOGING:
Arroyo, Jr., John, M.. (John M. Arroyo, Jr.)—Author
Corvin, Jr., Stan (Stan Corvin, Jr.)—Co-Author
Attacked at Home: A Green Beret's Survival Story of the Ft. Hood Shooting
201 pages 23cm × 15cm (9in. × 6 in.)
DESCRIPTION: "Attacked at Home: A Green Beret's Survival Story of the Ft. Hood Shooting" is the story about Second Lieutenant John M. Arroyo, Jr. who on April 2, 2014, while walking to his headquarters building on Fort Hood, Texas, was shot in the throat and neck by another soldier who then went on to kill four soldiers, including himself, and wound sixteen others. "Attacked at Home: A Green Beret's Survival Story of the Ft. Hood Shooting" also is about Arroyo's life beginning with his childhood in Southern California including his time spent as a tattooed member of a violent street gang, a hopeless teenage drug addict and then his enlistment in the U.S. Army where he ultimately becomes a Special Forces Green Beret and highly decorated officer after serving two tours of duty in Afghanistan and one in Iraq. The book also tells how Arroyo uses his Christian faith to protect himself and his fellow Special Forces "Operators" while deployed to the Middle-East and then relies on it to recover from the massive wounds he sustained after being shot on Fort Hood, Texas.

ATTACKED AT
H⊕ME!

a GREEN BERET'S
SURVIVAL STORY *of*
the FORT HOOD
SHOOTING

CAPTAIN JOHN ARROYO, JR.
U.S. ARMY (RET.)

With Stan Corvin, Jr.
Author of *Vietnam Saga*

DEDICATION

This book is dedicated to those who grew up without a father or mother or even worse; both parents. Those who find, or found, themselves so lost in addictions they cannot see a glimmer of hope that things will change for the better. Those whose homes were, or still are, a battleground. Those who have been told, "You will never make anything of your life. You're not smart enough. You're not good-looking enough. You're not good enough." Those whose hearts have been so broken it hurts to breathe; it hurts to live! And those who have been wounded by someone they trusted. Angel and I want you to know that we are telling our life stories because what is written in this book actually happened to us. Perhaps you can relate.

But that is not who we are today! We are no longer defined by our past. We are more than overcomers; we are conquerors. In this book is the hope you have been searching for. Because we endured so much tragedy, as you will soon read about and lived to share our healing with others, there is hope for you.

With that said,
Angel and I dedicate this book to **YOU!**

John M. Arroyo, Jr.

CONTENTS

FOREWORD

On April 2, 2014, I was sickened at the thought of more soldiers being killed and wounded by one of their own who was wearing the same uniform.

After the phone call, I sat there thinking, "*Is this going to be as bad as the first one that happened in 2009?*" I knew from previously going to Fort Hood that active shooter training was something that was an ongoing exercise at the hospital.

One of the cases the staff talked about was Lieutenant John Arroyo's, and they described his neck wound and the massive damage that had been done by the bullet. They also told me about some resources that had been in the right place at the right time for him. It just so happened that at the time, several ear, nose, and throat (ENT) doctors were training at the hospital, and they had completed a routine surgery. When the PA system announced "*Incoming critically injured patients,*" they immediately rushed to the emergency room. Also, an emergency room residency program was in place, and all of those personnel were there. So, we had the perfect types of teams in place to quickly respond to the situation. Having the right surgeon available when John was brought in, saved his life because he knew immediately what to do as John was bleeding out.

Walking down the wide corridor at Baylor Scott and White hospital, I was uneasy about seeing 2nd Lt. John Arroyo for the first time because I knew what kind of damage a large caliber gunshot wound can do to human flesh. I had seen it before in Kosovo and as an emergency room nurse! Having already been briefed on his condition earlier in the day at Darnall Army Hospital in Fort Hood, Texas, I knew that he had suffered a massive injury to his left carotid artery, larynx, and right shoulder from a .45 caliber bullet fired at almost point-blank range. It was a miracle that he was still alive after losing such a large amount of blood!

Gently knocking on John's door to announce my presence, I opened it and was astonished to see him sitting up in his bed, trying to talk and holding a whiteboard! Looking at the faces of his family standing around the bed, I saw their hearts were broken, and their lives had been shattered. I choked up as I entered the room, met everyone, and went over and hugged John. Then I said, "We are going to do everything we can to help you heal, and there's no limit to the resources we can offer. I would like to move you to San Antonio for your recovery." John awkwardly grinned at me and then wrote on the whiteboard, "Can I ride down there with you in your van?" And I just started laughing because that's the way John was! I could tell that he was not going to let this incident defeat him. That's when I realized that his faith and spirit was going to get him through this. Many people would simply have given up but not John; he was concerned about everybody else that had been involved in the shooting and how they were doing.

I had seen many soldiers with horrible injuries recover and go back on active duty because they didn't want to leave the military. I knew that John had the same desire, and I was sure that he would fully recover. His will to live was so strong it was apparent that after being shot, he had thought, *"Today is not my day to die!"*

Several months later, John was notified that he was going to receive the "Soldiers Medal." I was humbled and honored to be able to present it to him. During the attack, even though he was gravely injured and bleeding out, he had the presence of mind and resiliency to tell others about an active shooter in the medical brigade headquarters. His action that day saved many lives because others would have walked into the building and been killed by the shooter.

When somebody enters the military, they may or may not have come from a good home; however, very quickly, their brothers and sisters in uniform become closer to them than their actual family. A lot of John's strengths came from his wife, Angel, and he would not have been able to recover without her loving care. Her dedication to him and her daily attendance at his bedside was inspirational for everyone that knew her.

Being part of the United States military requires strength of character and commitment of purpose. As John and Angel have journeyed through the aftermath of a horrific attack, they have shown they possess both qualities, which will bring healing to many of those going through similar tragedies. I believe ***Attacked at Home: A Green Beret's Survival Story of the Fort Hood Shooting*** will become a shining beacon of light to show the path to recovery, health and restored hope for all who read it.

Major General Jimmie O. Keenan, U.S. Army (Ret.)

†††

CHAPTER ONE

California Living

Every strength I possessed was required of me to be able to survive the attack on April 2, 2014. There were many circumstances and influences that had shaped me into the man I was that day, and while they may seem unrelated, those childhood incidents proved to be a foreshadowing of things to come. The formative years began on September 10, 1977, when I was born in Montebello, CA. Later my family settled twenty miles southeast of Los Angeles in the city of Whittier, where I grew up. From the time I can remember, my parents were separated. The separation must have happened only a year or so after I was born because I do not remember shopping or going on outings with both of them. I grew up with my mom Rose Marie and grandmother Rosie. She moved in with us along with my sister Donna who is five years older than me, and brother Steve, who is one year older than me.

Grandma Rosie helped by watching us and making sure we stayed out of trouble. In those days, kids played outside and didn't come home until dinner. On Sunday morning, when the church bus blared its horn, kids and families loaded up to receive the "Good News." One Sunday, when I was about four years old, I had gotten up before the rest of the family and was watching cartoons on TV. The loud church bus horn sounded and thinking nothing about still wearing my pajamas, I got on the bus. Arriving at church, the ladies helping with the children called my house—letting my mom know I was at the church. She came and got me and scolded me for leaving home without telling her or my grandmother.

Experiencing unexpected, life-altering events started early in my life. As a very young boy, I often slept with my mom. You could say I was a momma's boy. I remember on Thursday, October 1, 1987, to be exact, I cozied up close to my mom before I got out of bed, gave her a kiss on the cheek, told her I loved her, then suddenly something happened. A 5.9 Richter scale earthquake hit our city. Not sure what was going on, everyone in our apartment remained silent as the building shook violently. Once it stopped, we all ran outside, afraid the apartment complex would collapse. We were later told the earthquake lasted for approximately twenty seconds. The aftershocks continued for several days. Of course, everyone was now waiting for the big quake that would make California an island and separate us from the other forty-eight states. That did not happen, but nearly everyone in our complex slept outside for a few days until we dared to go back inside permanently. Eight people in the city lost their lives as a result of the quake, and there was an estimated $360 million in property damage in the community.

On Saturdays, I walked with Grandma Rosie to Saint Mary's Catholic Church, which was where most people in our community attended. We stood in a long line at their weekly food bank and always walked away with the infamous four-pound block of cheese. That cheese made many quesadillas in our house—especially late in the month when money was running low, and making a meal took a bit of creativity with what was available in the refrigerator and pantry. My grandmother taught our entire family, including me, about Jesus as she had us attend services. I didn't understand the messages at the time, but as I look back—that experience was spiritual seed planting time.

Early every night, Grandma would go to bed, but she didn't immediately go to sleep. She would pray for our family for several hours before finally shutting her eyes. Her closeness to Jesus Christ then has now become the standard for my relationship with Him today. It was never about religion with Grandma; it was about a relationship. I believe there was a hedge of protection placed around my family because of the "effective fervent prayers" of my grandmother. Later, when I started my own family, I thought back to Grandma Rosie and our conversations about Jesus and how His blood was shed for me. I knew it was my responsibility to introduce my children to Him, so I would take them to church at Fort Bragg, NC. I cannot tell you that everything was perfect when we left the church, but today as I have conversations with my children, I believe those days were foundational opportunities for them to grow spiritually. My children have Jesus in their lives because of the faith seed Grandma planted in me, and I placed in them.

Although my father was active in our lives, his life was cut short due to cirrhosis of the liver. My mother told us when he was a young boy, his uncles gave him alcohol so they could laugh and be amused by his drunken antics. What they didn't know is that they were planting evil seeds of destruction as well. What was supposed to be a joke and funny ultimately caused more sadness than joy. My family and I were deprived of his presence and love because of what his uncles thought was funny. My parents divorced, and my siblings and I lost our father when he was in his early thirty's because of alcohol.

I have vague memories of my father, who was named "Juan." (Spanish: John) My mother named me John, but my birth certificate states I am "John Jr." Later, when my son was born, I wanted him named after me, so he is a "Junior" as well. I don't have a lot of memories of my father because I was quite young when he died, but there were a few that come to mind. I remember running races with my brother as my father refereed. One time my brother wanted to do something nice for my father. There was a convenience store across from my father's house, and the owners knew us well from going in and out with my dad. One day my father gave my brother a few dollars to buy sodas and some candy. My brother returned home and said, "Dad, I got you something." He handed my father a can of beer. My father was confused, saying, "Where did you get the beer from? My brother said, "I bought it for you at the store." My father was quite shocked. He didn't know whether to be mad or glad. He called my mom and said, "Steven, just bought me a beer." I'm sure my father thought it was a nice gesture, but he still talked with the store clerk and told him to never sell us any beer.

My father was also very protective of his children. One day several men from the neighborhood drove by and stopped at the curb next to me and said. "Hey, Lil John, would you like to go for a ride." I thought, "How cool." So I got in their car, and they drove me around the block and returned to the front of my father's house and yelled to him, "Juan, you want your son?" My father snatched me out of that car faster than you can imagine. He told me to wait inside for him as he had a few harsh words with those men. When he came in the front door, I heard what every kid dreads; the sound of leather sliding through belt loops. My father gave me a harsh spanking that I still remember today. But he did it out of love. What I didn't know was that those men who drove me around the block were well known, vicious gang members.

A year or two before my father died, he met a woman and began a romantic relationship with her. A funny thing happened the first time my mother realized my father had moved on from their marriage. One day he stopped by our apartment building with his new girlfriend for a visit and to deliver some groceries. I don't remember how the argument started, but I do remember that my mom was not happy there was another woman with him, so she proceeded to let my father know how unhappy she was by throwing the milk that he had just delivered at my father's car. I remember everyone yelling, "Not the milk!"

After Dad died, mom did her best raising us. She went to cosmetology school and soon started cutting and styling hair for most of our friends and family. We didn't have much money at all, but Grandma pitched-in from her Social Security check, and we received a small amount from my father's Social Security benefit.

Our home was filled with love, and we received frequent hugs from my mom and grandmother. The neighbors and close friends also looked after us as if we were their own flesh and blood. Occasionally, Mom or Grandma sent us to ask a nearby neighbor if we could borrow extra spice, sugar, or a cup of milk for the meal they were preparing; and they never judged us. At dinner, we had many animated conversations with one another when Grandma whipped up a restaurant-style meal, which I always wondered how she did that because when I looked in the refrigerator, I only saw milk, lard, and Tapatio hot sauce.

I never realized we were at the lowest end of family incomes and were near the poverty level for our nation. One reason why it never occurred to me that we were poor was that everyone I knew lived about the same as we did. Many of you will likely be able to relate to what I'm about to say. Our neighborhood, although poor, was a close community where everyone looked out for each other.

My middle name is Manuel, and frequently at home, I was called that, but at school, the teachers referred to me by my first name, John. When my friends visited, and someone from my household called me "Manual," my friends would say, "Who is Manuel?" I was a bit embarrassed at first, but then it just became the norm. I am seventy-five percent Mexican and a twenty-five percent Puerto Rican, which equates to a whole lot of confusion. My grandmother and mother knew and spoke Spanish to each other but never shared it with us, so we grew up culturally as Hispanics but not really knowing the Spanish language.

As I said, I grew up in a home with lots of love. That love was also extended to the neighborhood kids that frequented our home, and it was kind of a cool place to hang out. However, neither drugs, nor drinking was allowed, so our home was a safe haven for everyone. The kids in the neighborhood called my grandmother, "Grandma." We couldn't go anywhere without someone yelling "Grandma" from a car driving by or in an aisle in the supermarket.

Grandma was a faithful Catholic, but I'm not sure how she came to believe in Jesus. In my family, it seemed being Catholic was expected; you just were one. Although Jesus's mother Mary and several of the disciples are prominent figures in the Catholic faith, Grandma never talked to me about them. From my earliest memories, she only shared about the Trinity: Father, Son, and Holy Spirit. Grandma made sure we attended Saint Mary's Catholic Church. I do not want to mislead you into thinking we were regular church attendees because we were not, but we did attend the Christmas service, Palm Sunday, Ash Wednesday, and Easter service at a minimum. Each evening before going to bed, I would walk by Grandma's room and hear her praying. She was, indeed, a spiritual intercessor for our family.

I also had someone besides Grandma Rosie to share Jesus with me. It was Auntie Mary, my father's younger sister. Before passing away, he occasionally would pick up my brother Steve and me for weekend visitations. I don't think my father had much at his house to keep two young boys busy or entertained, so he took us to Auntie Mary's home in Covina, California. The drive to her house was only about thirty minutes, and I remember how excited I was to go there. We often traveled the scenic route from Whittier over Colima road past Turbo canyon through Hacienda Heights and La Puente then into Covina. I knew every landmark en route to Auntie Mary's house.

She had three kids my brother and I looked up to; Randy, the oldest, Trisha, the middle child, and Shelly, the youngest. They had a beautiful Golden Retriever named Sandy. If Sandy wasn't in the back yard, she was likely in the field behind their house chasing cats or rodents.

Auntie Mary mainly loved two people: Jesus Christ and Elvis Presley. She attended Calvary Chapel in West Covina, where Raul Ries was the Pastor. Currently, Pastor Ries and his church are in Diamond Bar, California. The church is now known as Calvary Chapel Golden Springs, with an average attendance of twelve to fourteen thousand people weekly. When we came over to visit, Auntie Mary would take us to church on weekends. This was the early 1980's when police officers weren't pulling people over for not wearing seat belts. We would pack in her car like sardines and head to church. My brother Steve dubbed her vehicle, "The God Squad Mobile." We still laugh about those days. At church, Auntie Mary was more charismatic than Grandma Rosie. She would shout, clap, and jump for the Lord. Every time she saw me, she'd say, "Manny, who loves you?" I would reply, "Jesus." I guess we don't always realize the spiritual seeds that are being sown into our children's lives, because Auntie Mary was right, it is Jesus who loves me, and you as well! When I was young, Jesus revealed Himself to me through Grandma Rosie and Auntie Mary. Today, He speaks right to my heart. Now I have taken on the role of Grandma Rosie and Auntie Mary by sowing spiritual seeds into those around me.

On one visit to Auntie Mary's, it was my turn to bathe before going to bed after a long day of playing outside. I took a bath, got out, but after drying off, I was itching all over. I thought it would go away, but it did not. Finally, I said, "Auntie Mary, what kind of soap do you have in the bathtub because I cannot stop itching?" My cousins looked at me a bit puzzled, and then Auntie Mary asked me, "Which soap did you use." I went into the bathroom and grabbed the soap bar and said, "This one." Everyone began to laugh, Auntie Mary did too, then she said, "That's our dog, Sandy's soap." Apparently, my cousins had given Sandy a bath earlier that day, and her soap wasn't removed from the tub area. I never lived that one down. Today I am over forty years old, and I still get reminded about bathing with Sandy's soap. Those were some fun times for sure!

My sister Donna was my parent's first child and the first grand-child for my mother's parents. She was a "Grandma's girl" spoiled, to say the least. So much so, that all my sister had to do was plead with Grandma, and she would get her way. Because Mom's cosmetology school started early, Grandma was in charge of making sure the kids were at school on time. On several occasions, Donna did not want to go to school. Mom and Grandma are not really tall women, so spankings were not a real threat to us. But once in a while, Donna would push Grandma to her limits. She had Whittier High School's security staff telephone number memorized, and they knew my grand-mother. So, Grandma would call Mr. Valenzuela and another school security staff member, Phil. Once the call was made, it usually went something like this, "Mr. Valenzuela, Donna, does not want to go to school today." In a few minutes, the two security guards would knock on our door, "Okay, Donna, let's go." My sister would be mad, but she couldn't fool those guys.

As young boys, my brother and I loved riding our bikes and skateboards. We stayed out for hours with our friends riding all over the city, often times leaving early in the morning and returning in the evening or just in time for dinner. Back then, there was not a lot of crime and gangs in the area. I am sure danger was around us, but my grandmother prayed, and the Lord protected us. Many times we went to City Hall's multi-storied parking garage. Walking to the upper parking level, we would skateboard down its exit ramp at high rates of speed. We never wore any protective gear, and thankfully no one was ever injured.

When we weren't out riding through the city streets, we had a route where we raced each other. The starting point was the front of our apartment complex. Then it turned right at J.G. Park and the school district buildings, turned right at Arthur's house, up to the front of Whittier High School, and finally a right turn at Bob's Auto and back to our apartment building. It was a fun course, but it wasn't without its share of dangers. We had to contend with lots of traffic, especially since Bob's Auto mechanics were usually test-driving vehicles up and down the street after they were repaired.

On one occasion, my brother was riding a ten-speed bike on our short track course, something he had done for many years. But, for him, this one loop changed things forever. As he rounded J.G. Park heading towards Arthur's house and made the turn towards Whittier High School, he was hit by a car. The collision was heard by nearby neighbors. One of the ten-speed's pedals gouged into my brother's shin, exposing his bone. I remember frantic knocks from a neighbor as they tried to reach my mom and Grandma to tell them about the accident. My brother received a skin graft to replace the skin where the pedal had cut his shin. He wore a cast for a few months but finally recovered quite well.

Although I do not have a lot of memories with my father, I do remember him picking me up and taking care of me while my mom was with my brother in the hospital. My father took me to McDonald's en route to visit my brother. After the accident, my father sternly would tell us, "Boys, stay out of the street."

Back then, the skateboarding scene was very popular, as well. Tony Hawk and Powell Peralta were professional skateboarders and had their own manufacturing facilities, and I attempted to skate like them.

I remember my first skateboard. It wasn't the *Back to The Future* skateboards that most kids had during that time. It was a Tony Hawk board with bones wheels and independent trucks. For a family on barely a subsistence budget, it took my mother about six months to pay off the skateboard's cost of $150 on a layaway plan. For us, that was a lot of money. I remember going to the skate shop every few days and asking the owner if I could see my skateboard. I'd even take my friends and show it to them. I did not become a skateboarding sensation, but I had a lot of fun skateboarding with everyone.

The weekend my father passed away, our phone had been disconnected because the phone company made a billing mistake. Those days were before everyone, including kids, had mobile phone devices. I recall my dad's younger sister came to our house early one morning. When my aunt knocked on the door, everyone was still wearing pajamas. There was a silence when she walked through the door. I think my mother was standing on the steps that led upstairs, my sister Donna was just a few steps below my mother.

My aunt said, "We've been trying to call you guys." My mother explained the mix-up by the phone company, and then silence filled the room. Finally, my aunt quietly told the news she dreaded to deliver, "Juan died!" Immediately I heard my sister Donna yell out with a loud cry. Throughout the house, everyone began to cry. As a young child, I did not understand what death was. All I knew was that my father was gone, and I would never see him again.

Quietly sobbing by myself, I thought, *"Who am I going to call when I meet a young girl, and who is going to talk with me about the "birds and the bees?"* Growing up, I saw my friends and their fathers together. I always questioned what characteristics I possessed that came from my father. My brother is a natural mechanic, and can easily take engines apart and put them back together again; that is a quality from my father. At the time, I did not know how much of my identity I lost when he died. My aunt told us, as my father was dying, he kept calling out for my mother and sister, who were the loves of his life. She also said he was having visions of my brother and me getting too close to the street because my father was calling for my brother and me to stay out of the road. My father entered eternity with his family in his heart. Now that I am older than my father was when he died, I frequently look in the mirror, wondering if I look like him.

When my brother had his accident, break dancing was a big deal for us. We watched the 1984 movie, *"Breakin."* We should have bought the movie because we rented it nearly every weekend for six months. The movie characters were Kelly, a classical jazz dancer who becomes friends with two break-dancers, Ozone and Turbo. Everyone wanted to break-dance like them. We would find cardboard sheets and spin on our heads and perform what is known as the windmill, where you tuck your arms in and spin your body with your legs extended as you rotate, thus giving the impression of a windmill. Several of my friends carried the big ghetto blaster radio with a cassette tape playing dance music. I still remember my brother attempting to break-dance while on crutches. We have pictures of him moving his arms all kinds of ways, getting his dance moves going.

Before I go any further, I have to mention someone near and dear to my heart, my best friend in the whole world, Arthur. He and I met in elementary school. I recall us throwing sand on each other one time, and then I said, "You want to be my friend?" And a friendship was born. Throughout my early life, Arthur was always by my side. We made a covenant with each other and said, "We may have other friends, even good friends, but we will always be best friends!" Sadly my best friend died sooner than any of us expected; however, our covenant stands today.

Gang Banger Influence

Whittier is quite large and sprawling, and I grew up in what we called "uptown" Whittier, which is an area concentrated with small shops and restaurants. Several movies were filmed in our community: *"Back to the Future Part I"* with Michael J. Fox. The scene where George McFly punches Biff in the face and rescues his date and goes on to the dance was filmed at my alma mater Whittier High School. The 1987 movie *"Masters of the Universe"* with Dolph Lundgren as the courageous warrior He-Man was partially filmed in uptown Whittier.

When I entered junior high, many of my friends and I began to get very territorial over our communities and neighborhoods. Until I was in sixth grade, I did not know anything about gangs. The street gang that claimed the area where we lived was the "Whittier Varrio Locos (WVL's)." The majority of my friends who I grew up with joined WVL's. But, as new teenage boys and girls moved into town from different parts of Los Angeles, they brought with them affiliations to the gang where they grew up. I planned to choose to join the WVL's, but that did not happen. A young man who had moved from Santa Fe Springs, which is approximately five miles from where we lived, was affiliated with a local gang there called the Canta Ranas (CR), which means "Singing Frogs." Because of his "cool" style and good looks, this young man had a lot of influence on Arthur and me.

Arthur and I both were "jumped" (initiated) into CR. Almost immediately, our lives went from being free to walk the streets to near-total seclusion in our own neighborhood. The two gangs, CR and WVL's, began to clash in deadly conflicts. I walked to school with no problem, mainly because most gang members were still sleeping, but after school was a different story.

In my eighth-grade year, I fought on and was chased through the streets I once called home. Frequently, I walked my girlfriend home (later, my son's mother and my first wife). I carried her books, and we would be talking about our day: when a rival gang would see me. They usually were driving past with four to five guys packed in a car. I was outnumbered, so I gave my girlfriend her books and took off running. If the fight were one-on-one or maybe even one against two, I considered staying, but frequently I was outnumbered, and I was only fourteen years old. I wasn't capable of fighting four or five guys armed with switchblades and guns all at once.

Several of the neighborhood guy's joined WVL's and had a lot of influence in the gang, so one day, Grandma called them over to the house for a chat. As I previously mentioned, everyone loved Grandma. She used her power to keep me safe. The gang members from WVL's knew where my grandmother lived and also knew that the house was off-limits to them. When I got chased, getting home to Grandma was my goal, and it became a deadly game of cat and mouse.

One evening Arthur and I were walking near Saint Mary's church, which was only two streets from our apartment complex. We were talking about his girlfriend and mine when a car packed with members from WVL's saw us, about the same time we saw them. Within seconds the tires from their car began to burn out and squeal, and they changed their direction back towards Arthur and me. We took off and ran for safety. Arthur quickly found a hideout. As I ran past him with one of the WVL's only a few feet behind me, Arthur called out to me, "John come in here." But, I kept running, not wanting to reveal Arthur's position knowing I was being pursued by one WVL on foot and the rest in the car. I quickly began to outrun the one on foot. Then the vehicle picked him up, and the chase continued.

On the corner where my brother and I rode our bikes, I ran out of breath, and the car caught up with me. A passenger in the car jumped out with a handgun, ran to me, and pointed it in my face. Bending over and breathing heavily, I froze as he got within inches of my face with the gun barrel. He squeezed the trigger, but no round fired. I heard him curse and slap the handgun, but this time, I wasn't sticking around to see if his second attempt to kill me would be successful. I ran with everything in me, and when I got within shouting distance, I yelled, *"Grandma!"* I stopped running when I got to the driveway of our apartment complex. The car followed and came to a skidding stop in front of me. I thought, *"This is it. They have me."* The car doors flew open, and everyone inside began to jump out and run towards me, ready to shoot and end my life. But out of nowhere, one of my neighbors happened to be walking out of his apartment and yelled loudly, "Hey, what are you doing!" He must have startled the guys who were chasing me because they all stopped and then ran back to their car and sped off. I now look back over that event and see Jesus's hand was on my life even then because I should have died from that encounter. A few days later, I saw a group of guys I had never seen before gathered at the front of my apartment. These gang members were very hostile, and looking to challenge and fight guys I grew up with and knew. That event was just another example of gang violence right on my doorstep.

Several years earlier, a friend of mine from elementary school had moved away. I didn't know what happened to him, but a female friend I knew stayed in contact with him. I often asked her about Robert. Then one day, he happened to be visiting some mutual friends of ours when our paths crossed, and everything about his appearance had changed. He was dressed like a gang member. So, what does that look like? For the most part, gang members wore oversized Dickies° jeans or shorts, t-shirts, and white tube socks to their knees, and a pair of Nike° Cortez shoes.

Several of the girls in our group were attracted to the ways of gang members. As a young, naïve kid, I really didn't know the dangers of being in a gang. All I remember is that girls liked it, and it was a new thing! I talked my mom into buying me Dickies° and Nike° Cortez, and little by little, I began to conform to what I thought was a very cool appearance. I remember my brother calling me one day and warning me to be careful because word got back to him that I was hanging around with gang members. Previously, for a short time, he had joined a gang, and now his little brother was beginning to follow in his footsteps.

To be honest, I wasn't one of your hard-core or extreme gang members. I was more laid-back. What's strange to me now is that I joined a gang located in a neighboring town rather than where I grew up. That decision led to conflict between my childhood friends and me. Often I was chased by rival gang members through streets I knew very well, and many times, I was unable to walk in some areas of the city for fear of gang violence.

Towards the end of our eighth-grade year, we found out my girlfriend, Andrea, was pregnant, and we were very scared. We didn't want to tell anyone. But, we couldn't hide her pregnancy for long. One day my sister Donna told my mother, "Mom, I think Andrea's pregnant." When confronted, however, I denied it emphatically saying, "No, she is not." We told everyone she gained weight from staying in the house over the summer. My mom believed me. But, the truth always comes out, especially in the case of a pregnancy. Eventually, we had to tell someone, so Andrea broke the news to her Aunt Cindy and Uncle Bobby. Then I had to tell my mom. We needed support because, at the time, we both were only fourteen years old. When I broke the news to my mom, she sat down and said, "I feel like I was just hit with a ton of bricks." That was the only time I was thankful I did not have to face my father. Although we shared the truth with Andrea's Aunt Cindy, we did not break the news to her grandmother, even though she was living with her. But, it would not be long before my son "Junior" would make his appearance, and the world would know the truth. As I write this, it shocks me. I cannot believe my son was born only twenty days after my fifteenth birthday. I look at fourteen-year-old kids today and think, "I cannot imagine you with a baby."

We started our freshman year at Whittier High, and I signed up for two extracurricular activities: band and football. Okay, go ahead and laugh; a gang member who was in the band and played football. Have you ever seen the movie *"Stand and Deliver?"* This story centers on a classroom of students who are average in their academics at best but go on to ace California's advanced calculus exam with the help and dedication of their teacher, Mr. Escalante. One of the students, "Angel" (played by Lou Diamond Phillips), was torn between a life as a gang member and his life in academics. My four years in high school were similar to Angel's. While at school, my friends were mainly people I grew up with from elementary through high school, and none were gang members. But, when I walked off campus, my backpack came off, and the gang member came out.

Fortunately, I had a teacher from my eighth-grade year at Dexter Middle School who never gave up on me. He was the school's band director, and he also taught history. I respected Mr. C., and I did not want to let him down, so when he asked me to join the high school band, although I did not really want to, I agreed. When I began my freshman year, band practice started at 7:00 am, and classes at 8:10 am. Because Andrea was pregnant, I walked her to school then showed-up late to band practice. The teacher never said anything; however, he did not allow me to participate in any field exercises during varsity football games.

Andrea was doing well in school, but because we were hiding her pregnancy, and none of the teachers had been told, she was required to participate in physical education (PE). On September 29th, 1992, Andrea was approximately six months along in her pregnancy, and her PE teacher had her class run up and down several flights of stairs for exercise. The next morning on September 30th, Andrea called me saying that she had not slept, and her stomach had been hurting all night. I said, "Call your Aunt Cindy and see what she says." Aunt Cindy advised that we needed to get to the hospital right away. Aunt Cindy and Uncle Bobby picked us up from Andrea's apartment complex and took us to Presbyterian Hospital in Whittier. Uncle Bobby and I went to the Emergency check-in window, saying, "We have a young woman who is pregnant with severe stomach pains." It took several minutes to check her in, then they took her back for evaluation. It didn't take long for the doctors to realize Andrea was in labor. I called my mom and family and had them come to the hospital. My mom had just arrived when the hospital intercom began sounding an alarm, **"Code Pink! Code Pink! Code Pink!"** I didn't know what that meant, but real fear rose up inside me. Frankly, I began to cry, fearing the worse and wondered, "Is Andrea, okay?" Soon, the doctors came out to the waiting area and told me that Andrea had delivered our son. Apparently, we arrived at the hospital just in time because when she was assigned to a room, and the doctors began their evaluation, her water broke, and within minutes, she delivered the baby. Sadly, she had been in labor by herself all night. Thankfully, Jesus's grace was with us, and our son was safely born; however, the baby's birth changed our lives.

We had to tell Andrea's grandmother, Victoria. Andrea's mother, Lisa, who did not live with Andrea and her grandmother, called Ms. Victoria and said, "Mom, are you sitting down?" Ms. Victoria said, "Why?" Lisa said in a shaky voice, "Because Andrea just had a baby." Ms. Victoria said, "What are you talking about? Andrea's in school." Lisa said, "No, Mom, she's at Whittier Presbyterian Hospital, she just had a baby boy."

Andrea's grandmother was not happy when she saw me. I remember that she walked passed me and said many derogatory things about what she thought of me. Thankfully, several of Andrea's family members and mine supported us. Because Junior was born prematurely, he had to stay in a hospital incubator for a month until his lungs developed, and he could be released. Ms. Victoria was not happy with Andrea and had her move in with her Aunt Diane near the San Bernardino area, which was approximately an hour away from Whittier. That might not seem far for most people, but when you are a fifteen-year-old kid with no car, it might as well have been in another state.

Sadly, over time, the distance was too far, and the drive affected my relationship with Andrea as well. We were two young kids trying to live like adults while in high school. In the end, it did not work. I have the utmost respect for Andrea and her achievements. She always excelled at academics; which is where Junior gets his intelligence. Even while raising a young son, she maintained straight A's in high school and then went on to college, where she received undergraduate degrees in graphic design and business.

During my freshman and sophomore year in high school, I did everything possible to be with Andrea and Junior. I nearly failed every course those two years because I was either absent, visiting Andrea and Junior, or sleeping in class. In the summer of my sophomore year, Andrea and I began having relationship problems. But, then something happened inside me, and today I know what it was. Holy Spirit kicked me in the pants and said, "Boy, God has great plans for you, so get your life in order, or you'll miss your destiny." I turned everything around and focused on my academics. My mother went to a parent-teacher conference, and the teacher asked, "What's happened to John?" Thinking something bad had happened, my mother replied, "I don't know. What do you mean?" Ms. Sawyer, my teacher, replied, "He is a different person." That year I began to receive awards for academic excellence and joined the computer academy, which no other gang member chose to do.

High school started as the happiest and the scariest time in my life. My son John Junior was born on September 30th, 1992. Simply put, we were kids having kids! How was I going to care for a kid? I couldn't even take care of myself? Thank God for my family and friends. My first two years of high school were kind of a blur because I was very immature. A lot was going on between my son's mom Andrea and me after she gave birth. When I attended a course, mostly, I was a distraction, wanting to be the class clown, frequently getting kicked out, and indeed denying myself an education. At the start of my junior year, I began to take school more seriously, signing up for computer courses and mentor programs. I received several awards and recognition for academic excellence, and for the first time in my life, I realized that I could do something with my life beyond being in a gang and chasing girls. Teachers began helping me, and that was new because I was usually a burden to them.

School relationships are powerful and can be both good and bad. The computer program that started my junior year had several students who, for two years, had been following my same path. There was a girl who caught my eye. We were just friends, but I found myself making sure I was at school to see her. I attribute much of my success in my junior and senior years to her. Although we were never formally in a relationship, she became much of the reason for my wanting to succeed in class.

Drug Addict

Have you ever done something foolish, and you immediately wished you could take it back? During my senior year, I tried methamphetamine for the first time. The meth I used was called "glass" and I assume it was called that because it appeared to be made of glass slivers. Ironically, this drug looks like broken glass shards, and its effect is to shatter lives. People who have experimented with this drug frequently have lost their families, jobs, relationships, and even their lives. Once I was exposed to this drug, it was tough to quit. I started off using meth on weekends. Initially, I didn't think I had a problem, but then I don't think anyone ever does.

I didn't graduate from high school in the traditional way by crossing the stage and receiving a diploma. I attended summer school, where I completed my final courses and then received my diploma. However, after school was over, the party didn't end; it simply intensified. Using meth didn't stay as a weekend thing; it crept into my daily life. During that time, I lied a lot to everyone as I tried to hide the addiction.

Soon everything began to fall apart. I was showing up late for work and staying up all night. I even lied to myself as I kept telling myself no one knew what I was doing. But that was a big lie. As a father, I was also failing! I frequently set a time to pick up my son then I would make an excuse why I couldn't. That caused serious conflict between his mother and me. I'd like to blame the drugs for much of my faults as a father, but I believe immaturity was a significant factor, as well.

My older sister quickly caught on to what I was doing. She actually had me move in with her and her husband so she could keep a close eye on me. She was able to see through my lies, and she called me out on them. If I stayed up all night, the next midmorning, she would pour water on me and say, "You are not sleeping all day." Finally, one day, she got fed up and knew there was nothing else she could do to help me. So she said, "Have you ever thought of joining the military?" Adding, "You need to get out of here, or you're going to be a loser the rest of your life." She saw that my life was going nowhere, fast.

The first time she mentioned the military, I really was not interested. But after being fired from my job, friends telling me things were getting out of control, and a couple of more drenching's of water, I knew I needed help. My first thought was, "I will become a Marine!"

I went to the Marine recruiters and even took the practice test. The recruiters sent me away and told me I needed to study before they would allow me to take the actual military aptitude test. Later, I stopped in at a Marine recruiter closer to where I grew up, and during the conversation, I mentioned I had gang tattoos. He said you cannot have gang tattoos in the Marine Corps, either get them taken off or cover them up.

I decided to have my cousin cover up my tattoos. He had his own portable tattoo studio consisting of a self-made tattoo gun and equipment. I told him to cover them up, but what I ended up with is what appears to be mostly black ink on my skin.

Needless to say, I never went back to the Marine recruiters. A few days later, I was introduced to an Army recruiter by an acquaintance. I thought, *"This guy doesn't know who I am, and he doesn't know I have tattoos."* He never asked, and I never said anything. So I began my journey to become a U.S. Army soldier. My recruiter gave me a few tips on how to take the military entrance exam. Unfortunately, on my first attempt at the actual test, I failed. Doubt started to creep into me, and I thought, *"Maybe this isn't for me because I'm not smart enough."* I was given a few months to prepare for my second attempt at the test. I passed the exam by one point. I think the minimum required score is 30, and I scored a 31. But if you had seen me that day, you would've thought I scored 100! That one point represented a new opportunity. Now, all the pieces of my life were brought together as I was being shaped and formed into the man I was to become.

John Tattooed Gang Member

John Gang Member

Granma

Granma and Donna

Junior and Me

†††

CHAPTER TWO

U.S. Army Enlistment

I was sworn into the U.S. Army in March 1998 and boarded a plane headed to Fort Jackson, South Carolina, for basic training on June 17, 1998. I was excited and a little scared. I remember a day or two after we arrived, everyone lined up in front of a row of phone booths, and we were allowed to call our family. Of course, being a momma's boy, I called my mom at our home. You can be a really hard-core person, but when you leave home for the first time, and you hear your mom's voice on the other end of the telephone, I'm saying hard-core goes out the window. As soon as I heard the sound of my mom's voice, a knot formed in my throat, tears began to run down my face, and I could barely even get the word "Mom" out of my mouth. I remember all the recruits walking away from their phone calls wiping their eyes.

I left California to escape drugs and to start over, this time with discipline. One day while in basic training, we were told to clean our barracks. I figured out a way where it looked like I was cleaning, but I was catching up on my rest. I remember lying under my bunk feeling as if my body was detoxing. Of course, I was eventually caught and punished by having to perform many extra duties.

When I enlisted and selected my military occupational specialty

(MOS), I chose a transport operator, i.e., truck driving. The majority of the men in my family were truck drivers. I planned to join the military, obtain a skill (truck driving), and some discipline, then return home after three or four years and get hired as a truck driver. After basic training, I was transferred to the motor transport operators' course in Fort Leonard Wood, Missouri. Everything seemed to be working out fine until the class which graduated before we did all received orders to go to Korea. A good friend of mine I met at the military in-processing station in Los Angeles had been with me since we left there. We both saw what happened with the Korea class assignments and were hoping this didn't happen to us. A few days later, one of the drill sergeants addressed our platoon and said, "Who wants to go airborne?" *"Airborne?"* I thought. I do not like heights. But then he said, "This assignment will likely send you to Fort Bragg, North Carolina, home of the airborne." I don't remember the details, but I knew North Carolina was somewhere in the eastern United States. I talked my friend into going airborne so that we didn't end up in Korea.

After Army truck driving school, lasting from late October to early November 1998, I was sent to Fort Benning, GA, to attend the U.S. Army airborne school. It was broken down into three segments: ground week, tower week, jump out of airplanes week, then graduation if you have not been hurt. The school had two tall metal structures, which were two-hundred-fifty foot towers. These towers are designed to simulate your descent once you are lifted by cables up to the top and then released. The parachute opens upon release, and the trainee steers it to the ground. Thank God the towers were not in operation when I went to airborne school. Honestly, I don't know if I would have been able to compose myself to complete the task of being lifted up to the top of the towers. I didn't mind jumping out of airplanes because most military aircraft don't have windows, so you don't have to see what's coming. You stand up, receive your jump commands, check the equipment, shuffle to the door, and jump out. However, I was proud that I conquered my fear of heights. It would be one of the many personal issues that I would overcome in my military career. As I look back now, I realize that I wasn't operating entirely on my own ability, but God had his hand on my life and was moving me to the calling He had for me. Also, my grandmother, who was a strong prayer warrior, had been praying for me, and I believe God answered her prayers as well.

My decision to go to airborne school paid off, and after graduation, my friend and I received orders to Fort Bragg, North Carolina, home of the U.S. Army Airborne units and Special Operations. Inprocessing there was quite unsettling for a young twenty-one-year-old soldier who had only left home a few months before. Nearly everyone said, "You know you are going to the 82nd Airborne Division, and you will be deployed overseas."

I was assigned to Delta Company in the division's Main Support Battalion (MSB). We were called the "Delta Dawgs," and we were proud of it. We walked with our heads held high. Although our leaders were tough on us, they were compassionate mentors and trained us as if we were young rangers. When you're twenty-one years old in the 82nd Airborne Division, you begin to believe your leaders when they say, "We are the best." In Delta, we became a family. We fought among ourselves like brothers and sisters in a large family, but we also had each other's back too.

One of the soldiers in my platoon, Spec. Four Smith was approved to join the Fort Bragg bull-riding team. Unfortunately, during one of his rides, he was thrown off the bull, it somehow stomped on his face causing severe damage to his eyes, and he lost his sight. At the time, he had been dating one of the women in our platoon, Specialist Trotter. While Smith was recovering in the hospital, several of us decided to go bowling at the "Airborne Lanes." In an effort to help cheer her up, we asked her to join us. Saturday evening after 7:00 p.m., the bowling alley transitioned to "exotic bowling," which means they dim the lights and turn on neon ones. It's was kind of fun, and we enjoyed it. Drinking a lot of beer while there, the dimmed lights and loud music made us feel as if we were in a dance club.

We were having a good time horsing around and challenging one other to see who could score the most strikes. The bowling alley was packed with soldiers from various U.S. Army units throughout Fort Bragg. In the 82nd Airborne Division, there were not any women assigned to the infantry and artillery units; they were all-male units. So, when women were around, especially when alcohol was being served, they could expect soldiers to flirt with them. This evening was no different, we had several women with us, so the single male soldiers near our lanes began to wander closer to us. One soldier, in particular, kept trying to flirt with Specialist Trotter. We were troubled with his actions because her boyfriend was recovering in the hospital, so we felt obligated to prevent any males from flirting with her.

I told the soldier who had been trying to hit on Specialist Trotter, "Please back off, she has a boyfriend." However, he refused to listen and kept coming back. I approached him again, and this time, he and I began to fight. As soon as his friends saw that he was in a fight, they jumped on me too. Later one of my friends, who had just rolled his bowling ball towards the pins, said, "I turned around to walk back towards everyone when all of a sudden I see several guys around you and then your feet flying up in the air. I ran towards you, leaped in the air, and began swinging." Our female soldiers began swinging their fists too and jumping on the backs of the opposing unit soldiers. Several of the women were punched in the face. It was a real brawl. Almost immediately, the bowling alley staff turned the lights on and called the military police (MP). It seemed like only seconds after the fight started that the MP's were yelling at everyone to exit the building.

My friend and I began to walk out. We noticed the MP's were grabbing all those involved. I was wearing a Dodgers jersey, which I quickly ditched, knowing the MP's would also be looking for me. When we reached the door, one of the MP's saw that I had been hit because I had a lump starting to form near my left cheekbone. The MP said, "Hey, you come here." I played dumb, "Who me?" "Yes," he said, "What happened to you?" I answered, "A fight started, and I tried breaking it up, then someone elbowed me." He said, "Just sit here for a moment, and we are going to take a victim statement from you, and then you can go." I gave my statement just a few feet from the guys who we were fighting with, hoping they wouldn't recognize me. The MP's let everyone in my unit go. Our opponents were still sitting on the curb, waiting for their chain of command to show up. I thought, *"This isn't going to be a good night for them."*

We tried not to tell anyone about what had happened, but it did not help that I had a big shiner (bruise) under my left eye. Monday morning at the mess hall, our company first sergeant, and my platoon sergeant walked straight to where I was sitting. He said, "So what happened this weekend?" He smiled at me, and the first sergeant glared into my eyes, saying nothing. I replied, "Nothing, some soldiers kept hitting on SPC Trotter." The first sergeant cut me off, "Did the MP's report you? I said, "No." He said, "Then you all better have won that fight!" He laughed and walked away. The first sergeant and the rest of our leaders were a bunch of warriors, and they trained us to fight for one another. As long as they weren't being called to the commanding general's office, they were glad we kicked some butt.

A soldier's first unit can make or break his career. I left home searching for discipline, and I found it! Our leadership required that at all times, we kept up our military bearing, physical fitness, and proficiency at our jobs and duties. The foundation of who I was later to become as a soldier was established in this unit.

When I left California, I thought I made a clean break from my past. I didn't know others had joined the army from California or other states and had grown up in the same environment. However, it wasn't long before I met several of those individuals. Initially, I tried to separate myself from them, thinking that I might fall back into my old habits. Life is filled with choices, and I quickly realized those people were not going to cause me to slip backward unless I allowed it to happen. Actually, the more time I spent with them, the more we became family.

One thing that usually happens with military units who spend the majority of their time together, training together, deploying together, going through hardships together, is they become like family and establish relationships that last forever. It is not uncommon to be closer to your brothers and sisters in uniform than your own flesh and blood relatives. Today many of my best friends are those who served with me in the U.S. Army.

After a year or so, I realized that I enjoyed being in the military. My initial aptitude scores were quite low, and I knew if I wanted to apply for a new career path, it would require higher scores. After I spoke with my leadership and shared my desire to improve my career, they allowed me to attend a course to raise my scores. There were two of us from my unit who attended this month-long course. I was studying hard, really putting my all into this course; however, the sergeant that went with me wasn't. When we finished the course, we took the final exam, and my score had increased from 92 to 115, but the sergeant had raised his scores by only two points.

Now that I had improved my scores, the doors were open to almost anything I wanted to do in the military. As a truck driver, we spent many days and nights transporting parachutes from the drop zone where the infantry units had left them to the rigger shed (parachute warehouse). Several of the soldiers in those units were rangers. The term "ranger qualified" refers to infantry soldiers who have graduated from the U.S. Army Ranger School. It is an intensely physical and mentally challenging leadership school focused on small unit tactics. Soldiers who are ranger qualified usually are top performers.

I thought to myself, *"How do I get into Ranger school? I want to perform at a high level and be called upon when my nation needs the very best."* So one day, I was assigned to help clean our headquarters. While in the office, I spoke with my company commander saying, "Sir. How do I get to Ranger school or on deployment?" This was in 1999 or 2000, and not much was going on, at least for my unit. He said, "Arroyo, you want to deploy overseas? Let me see what I can do for you." The next day at formation, suddenly, I heard the platoon sergeant say, "Arroyo get down and start doing push-ups until I tell you to stop!" While I was in the front-leaning-position, he said to me, "What are you doing talking to the company commander, telling him you want to deploy?" In those days, we rarely spoke directly with the company commander. Needless to say, I was doing push-ups for quite a while.

Special Forces Training

Fort Bragg was not only home of the airborne units but also of special operations, so I decided to see if I could become a Green Beret. These soldiers wear the distinctive "Green Beret," which dates back to 1961 when President John F. Kennedy authorized U.S. Army Special Forces soldiers to be distinguished from other units by wearing it. They are known for irregular warfare or unconventional warfare, foreign internal defense, special reconnaissance, direct action, and counter-terrorism. Green Berets typically operate in small detachments of twelve soldiers who are capable of training and equipping foreign militaries and/or guerrilla forces in leadership strategies and small unit tactics. They are often called upon to go into countries before local and regional conflicts escalate. When conventional troops are deployed, it's not uncommon for Green Berets to have already been operating there for several months.

At the time of my initial inquiry about going to Ranger school, I was told that truck drivers were not authorized to attend it because it was only for infantry soldiers. Fortunately, for me, Green Berets accept all military occupations specialties (MOS). Soldiers who are successful in being chosen after the Special Forces selection and assessment process is completed are trained in one of the four primary occupations during the qualification course; weapons, engineering, medics, or communications.

Now that I made the decision to try out for Special Forces training, I started telling everyone how I was going to attempt selection. I'm not sure if I was completely sold on the idea myself because I was somewhat scared, and I honestly didn't think I was smart enough nor had what it takes to complete the selection process and make it to the qualification course. Soldiers that become Green Berets are absolutely the top performers in the military and usually are well-educated.

I applied to attend selection, and I began it on September 10, 2001. The following day, which we all know as the worst terrorist attack on the United States, September 11, 2001, we were taken to a classroom at noon and briefed that a major terrorist attack, involving high-jacking commercial airliners, had just taken place in New York City, at the Pentagon and crashing one in an open field next to a wooded area in Somerset County, Pennsylvania. Since we had just begun our training the day before, we thought that what we were being told was part of the classroom scenario. Unfortunately, we were mistaken.

When we realized the terrorist attack information was no training scenario, but an actual attack, many of the attendees, asked to return back to their home units. Several units, such as the one I was in, the 82nd Airborne Division, are capable of sending troops anywhere in the world within eighteen hours or less. Many of the students didn't want to be left behind if their unit was deployed. The senior school leaders told us to relax and to focus on the task at hand because it would be a few weeks or even months before any units went anywhere, and if we wanted to be a part of what was going to happen in the future, we were in the right place at the right time. During the twenty-four-day selection process, we were completely shut off from the outside world. It wasn't until I completed the rigorous training that I realized the magnitude of the attack.

I finished the course and made it to the end but was not chosen and was sent back to my unit with an opportunity to return in six months. I remember finally turning my cell phone on. There were countless messages from close friends and my family, wondering if I was okay. The last anyone had heard from me was a few days before I left for Special Forces selection, then the terrorist attacks occurred, and no one had heard from me since. My family was worried that I had deployed as a response to the attacks. Fortunately, I was safe and made many phone calls to everyone. However, I had to return to my unit and tell everyone I wasn't selected.

I struggled with whether I was going to attempt selection again. Sometime after January 2002, a handful of my teammates were selected to deploy. The remaining were going to spend a month at the National Training Center (NTC) in California. My name was on that list as well, but I told my chain of command that I was going back to selection during that time, which was in May or June. So I submitted my packet for the second attempt at the selection; however, I wasn't really motivated to go through the physical misery again. In preparation for the second course, I trained a little but not as much as I had on the first attempt. During the next attempt, which was in November 2002,

I remember wanting to quit every day. However, something inside me wouldn't let me, I kept thinking about my children and family. Telling them I had quit would be far harder than the physical misery I was enduring.

In 2002 when I returned to Special Forces Selection & Assessment (SFAS), my fiancée, Angel, and I were dating. She was born and raised in Battle Creek, Michigan, and her parents: Robert and Sylvia, both now deceased, had four children; Angel being the second oldest. We were taking college courses at Fayetteville Technical Community College in Fayetteville, N.C., and had struggled through failed relationships. Neither of us was looking to meet anyone or begin a romantic relationship, but I think that's usually when it happens. Angel and I were in the same English course. On the first day, our instructor was going over the syllabus. When she reached the required material list, she asked, "Does everyone have a floppy disc where you can save your work." (It's an older version of a thumb drive or memory storage device.)

When the teacher asked that question, I realized I did not have a floppy disc. I raised my hand to tell the teacher that I did not have one. She addressed the entire class saying, "Does anyone have an extra floppy disc for this gentleman?" A young country looking, blond-haired, hazel-eyed girl, said, "I have one." Then she handed it to me. On another occasion, my car had broken-down. I was able to find a ride to school, but I was going to walk home for the return trip. I looked around for the blond girl, thinking, "She was nice, maybe she'll give me a ride home." I worked up enough courage to ask her. I really didn't want her thinking that I was a psycho who would take advantage of her. I approached her and asked for a ride, and without much hesitation, she said, "Sure." Thank God she said yes because I was about to walk a long distance back to my unit, or creep more people out by asking for a ride. Little did I know that girl who was generous enough to give me a floppy disc would one day become my wife. Funny thing is, after nearly sixteen years of marriage, I still have not replaced the floppy disc she gave me.

It wasn't until August 2003 that we married. Most people plan extravagant weddings; however, when you're an E-5 "Buck Sergeant" you're not making much money. But we had a beautiful wedding on a limited budget—we were happy, and that mattered the most! Additionally, at that time, I was the male role model for Angel's children Tia and Mason, who were living with us while I was training for my second attempt at Special Forces Assessment School. My son Junior and I frequently talked by phone, but I don't think he truly understood what I was signing up for. During SFAS and on into the Qualification Course (Q-Course), I knew that I had a lot to learn and that I might very well fail. But it wouldn't be from a lack of trying or quitting. If I did not become a "Green Beret," it wouldn't be because I didn't work hard enough.

I may not have excelled at many things, but I wasn't a quitter. When you quit something one time, it's easier to do it the next time, and I never wanted to start that trend. Fortunately, I was a bit more confident and was prepared mentally for what was ahead. At the end of the selection, roster numbers are called out, and candidates are divided into two formations. It doesn't take long to understand what's happening, which group are the selectee's and which group have to attend a board or are told to leave. Things were different now for me because I had a family nearby and was highly motivated, and I made it to the selected formation. During those twenty-four days, you put your body through a lot, and often you'd see candidates barely able to walk because their feet were in so much pain. But when I was selected, whatever pain I had was gone. Hallelujah!

I returned back to my unit and prepared to transfer to the qualification course, which started in March 2003. This course was geared towards infantry and special operations tactics, and it was a tough learning curve for me. We had done a lot of small unit tactics in basic training but nothing to the magnitude of where I now found myself. I had really good teammates that came alongside me and shared their knowledge. But at the end of the day, no one can do it for you, and you had to pull your own weight. I had one instructor tell me, "I honestly didn't think you would make it, but you pulled through okay."

After my first SFAS attempt, I decided I really liked the military, and I wanted to reenlist and continue my career for a few more years. However, I wanted to change my occupation to something more sought after in the private sector if I ever left the U.S. Army. To advance my career, most occupations required additional education, so I thought, "If you ever plan to truly advance in life, you need more education." What helped me with my decision was that my close friend Sergeant Tapia had reenlisted and received six months of college as a reenlistment incentive. Our first sergeant really liked him and wanted to ensure the Army didn't lose a great asset, so he made sure Sgt. Tapia got what he wanted; his education. We both grew up in California and had similar backgrounds.

When I spoke with the reenlistment sergeant, he said, "We can give you a semester of college, where you will go to school fulltime like a traditional student. The only requirements are: you have to maintain physical fitness, report to your chain of command daily, or whenever they require and be ready for random urine analysis testing." I said, "What! Is that it? Where do I sign up?" So, in exchange for receiving a semester of college at Fayetteville Technical Community College, from January 2002 thru May 2002, I gave Uncle Sam four more years.

John's College Graduation

John in 82ⁿᵈ Airborne Div.

†††

CHAPTER THREE

Afghanistan Deployment

On the day I left Fort Bragg, Angel, and the kids drove me to nearby Pope Air Force Base. We gave each other hugs and kisses, and they prayed for my safe return. It was mid-June 2004. I had been given several weeks' leave to get my affairs in order before I deployed to the Middle East, where I was to meet my unit for six months of combat operations. On the day I was deployed, I remember waking up that morning thinking, *"Will this be the last time I wake up in my bedroom?"* I didn't share my thoughts with Angel, Tia, or Mason because I didn't want to worry them. I went through the house, staring at family photos, and taking my fingers, walked them across the faces of my children and family. I laid down on the floor and let my Rottweiler, "Lucky," lay next to me. She was a daddy's girl, and each day when I returned home from work, I could always expect Lucky to be waiting for me at the door. This time, I was leaving for work, but there was no guarantee I was coming home. Truthfully, I was probably going to miss her more than she would miss me. Growing up, we never could afford any pets. Lucky was my very first pet. And she was my dog!

I ate breakfast with my family making mental notes of each one's facial expression, laughter, tears, and smiles. I called my son Junior, making sure that he knew how proud I was of him, and I told him how much I loved him. I also shed a few tears during that conversation but tried hard to keep my composure, not wanting to upset anyone. I made several final calls to my mother, my sister Donna, and Grandma Rosie in the final moments at home. It takes a special kind of person to be willing to leave their family and travel thousands of miles across the globe knowing they will be participating in an active war with no guarantee, they will return home.

I loaded up my two tough boxes that contained my military gear and clothing, along with a few photos of my family. Angel wanted to take pictures together before we departed for Pope Air Force Base, where I would board a C-17 Globe Master and fly to Ramstein Air Force Base in Germany before making the final leg into Kandahar, Afghanistan. I took photos with Angel, then Tia and Mason. It is a humbling moment to be standing in your living room, taking photos with your family, knowing you may never return. How do you plan for that? If you never return, what photos or memories can you leave your family and friends that will be memorable keepsakes?

While driving en route to Pope Air Force Base, I made sharp mental images of Angel and the kids by frequently looking at them, and I clung to each of their spoken words. I tried to keep the mood light by trying to be funny. As we entered the security checkpoint, my chest got a little tighter, and my palms began to sweat. I thought, "I have boarded many C-17 Globe Masters, but this time I won't exit with a parachute over one of the many drop zones on Fort Bragg. This might be a one-way ticket!" We arrived at the passenger terminal. I met with Frank, the guy in charge of the flight manifest. I'm not sure what Frank's last name or rank was because, in most Green Beret units, everyone typically calls each other by first names except for senior noncommissioned officers and commissioned officers.

When it was time to board, others that were joining me on the flight began to give their families final kisses and hugs. I did the same, looked into the eyes of my beautiful wife, and said, "Pray for me." I hugged Tia and Mason and told them how much I loved them. Every few steps, I would look back and wave; my throat knotted up inside me. I choked back the tears, not wanting anyone to see them, and then I walked up the steps of the airplane, praying that Jesus would bring me back to my family.

Angel Recalls First Deployment
Her Story

The drive to the airfield had been difficult. It is never easy to do what you know you must do when everything within you wants to stop this thing from happening. The four of us made attempts at small-talk, which only led to deeper silence. It was impossible to talk about the "big thing." John frequently took his attention away from traffic for a second to look at me. My face reflected what was in my heart and prompted him to say, "You'll be okay, I'll be back in only six months, don't worry about me." I nodded my acceptance of his words and concentrated on staying strong. Mason, Tia, and I managed to hold it together as we said our good-byes and watched as he walked to his assigned airplane.

For ten months, we had shared our married life with a deep measure of happiness, truly the most joy I had known up to that point in my life. Now questions rose up from my heart and flooded my mind. How would I handle it all again? I had been a single mother to my two children for many years, but now I was used to sharing that with John. How could I live with the loneliness again? Having John as a husband and the love we shared had shown me just how lonely I had been for my entire life. The chasm of loneliness, which was going to stretch out into my coming days, caused a sense of dread within my heart. Why did this military job of his have to take him away for such a long time? Thinking of my husband's deployment as a job was a way to protect myself from something I simply couldn't process emotionally at that point. "Battlefield" was a word I refused to accept into my thoughts. He was part of a highly trained team. They worked together and protected each other. They weren't like other soldiers who were sent out in large groups. He was one of a special team, and they did their job, looked out for each other, and then came back.

Standing at the airfield that day, the dam holding back all the thoughts, fears, and feelings broke when he boarded the plane that would take him to unknown places to carry out undisclosed missions that we would never fully know about or understand. As the door to the airplane shut and the engines roared to life, the depth of the pain within me roared to life as well. Mason, Tia, and I began to cry like babies! Unashamedly, unrestrained, and desperate to soothe this ache, we let the tears flow until we could cry no more. In silence, we drove back to the place we wanted to call home, yet knowing it would now be redefined. There is an old adage that states, "Home is where the heart is." When your heart just got on a plane flying to Afghanistan, it's hard to find your way back home.

The broken and rocky road of my life had led me through times of living in many different houses with many different people, but only after John and I found each other did I finally know what home really felt like. Sitting in the quiet house left in the wake of John's deployment gave me much time to reflect on my life.

Given the sheer odds, our meeting was nothing short of miraculous. John was raised in Southern California, and I was from Battle Creek, Michigan. In retrospect, the irony of the name of my birth city pierced my heart. My whole childhood had been a battle with my mother. I was the only one of her four children she honestly did not like. The older I got, the more she attacked me. By the time I was a young teen, her abuse had intensified, and there were frequent physical attacks. Whenever my father, who was my rock and my protector, left, her fury was unleashed. There were many times as I grew older and started fighting back that my younger sister called my Aunt Becky to come and break up the fight. She would come quickly, restrain my mother until she calmed down, and then take me with her to her house. My house was a battleground, but so was my Aunt Becky's house. Her husband physically and verbally abused her regularly, and while he never attacked me, my presence at no time kept him from acting out on his rage in awful ways toward my sweet aunt. I never could understand why my mother hated me so much. Anytime I raised the subject with my father or my aunt, they would try to reassure me that it wasn't really me my mother hated as they explained that she had wanted a son when I was born, so she was disappointed. But that didn't make any sense to me because my mother had two sons and two daughters, and I was the only one she hated.

When I was old enough to work, an opportunity to live with another family presented itself, and I quickly took advantage of the chance to leave home. I had met a single mom who needed help watching over her children and getting them to school in the mornings. With no formal announcement at home, I gradually moved in with her and then found an after-school job at a Burger King˚. She was grateful for the help and treated me like I was an adult, giving me no real supervision. This arrangement also gave me the freedom to search for a way to fill that empty space in my heart that longed to be nurtured and given love from my family; that place that was desperate to be filled. I soon found a high school sweetheart and a glimmer of what seemed to be love. At age seventeen, I dropped out of school, began working full time, and poured myself into trying to believe I had found a forever relationship. Two years later, on the day I told him I was pregnant, he told me he was a drug addict. We said our wedding vows, but in truth, he was married to his addiction. I married to have a way out of the battleground with my family and hoped that maybe my husband would choose to love me more than his drugs. Six years later, I realized that would never happen. During those years, I had given birth to a daughter and then a son; I had received my high school diploma and developed a strong work ethic. I was able to save enough to buy a house, but too many times to even begin to relate, I came home to find our television, or microwave, or something else gone. He would sell or pawn things we had and buy more of his first love - narcotics. In my mind, marriage was a "no-matter-what" proposition. It had to be that because it was what I had seen modeled in my family. If divorce were an option, surely my father would have left my mother when she was so abusive to him. It was only after a co-worker of mine, an older woman who had great wisdom and insight, "read my mail" and began to understand what I was going through that my path became clear. She encouraged me to find freedom through a divorce. She talked about God and His forgiveness and told me divorce could be forgiven in my situation if I asked God. I began to pray to a God I knew about but didn't have a relationship with simply because a woman who had a relationship with Him told me I could. After months of this, I finally felt peace, divorced my husband, and started a life on my own. It's interesting to reflect on that time and see that it didn't draw me closer to God. Instead, I traveled down a rocky path, still looking for the warmth of love in a cold and shattered world. That well-trodden path finally led me to a place of such despair that I gave up on life. Working two jobs, caring for two children, and completely overwhelmed with the pressure of just trying to hold it all together, I reached the point of acknowledging that my existence was not life. I made several attempts to end my shallow façade of existence. Ironically, my mother stepped in and took over the care of my children until I could heal physically and also emotionally through intense counseling. Another decade of brokenness and profound loneliness filled my life before I met the man who would change everything for me. A chance encounter in a classroom provided a moment with this man, coming from his own fragmented journey, who became my friend, my confidant, and ultimately the love of my life. We connected at that place within me that was desperate to love and be loved. And now he was across the world. It took intense effort for me to hold on to the tiny glimmer of hope he had given me.

His absence in our home was profound. I went through my days taking care of the details, managing the way I knew I had too, but always wondering if I was doing what John would want me to do. My son Mason and daughter Tia had been with me through all my chaotic life and emptiness, and I know they had felt the hope that John had brought into our lives. They were teenagers, and they both resisted our rules, deeming them too strict as most teens feel about their parents' rules. But I was mindful of their heartfelt tears as John left that day. The heart will find ways to express its deepest desire and sometimes uses diverse methods to do so.

Being part of the United States military truly meant I had a big extended family. During the next six months, we connected with other wives and children in a way I had never experienced before. No matter what our backgrounds, we all had a common bond. We understood each other's journey; everyone was willing to help anytime there was a need. We gathered socially; we did fun things together, and we didn't discuss the war. There was an unspoken understanding to focus on the "here" not the "over there," and we lived in the "now" of our day-to-day lives. We didn't dwell on the "what ifs," the "I wonder," and all the questions that none of us could answer anyway. And we watched! Fortunately, within John's group, there was never a time when we saw the saddest sight a military wife can witness. When an officer in formal uniform flanked by another service member who is usually a chaplain carrying a Bible, arrives at a home and walks toward the front door, silence falls on all the witnesses. Often, it is a notification of the death of the soldier, although it can also mean they are severely wounded or missing in action (MIA). The fact that we never witnessed this meant his team was alright. They were highly trained Green Berets, which strengthened my belief that nothing would ever happen to him.

Finally, the six months were up! It had seemed an interminable time, and I was filled with excitement to have my husband back. Our house would be home again, I could laugh, really laugh again. He was coming back and bringing "home" with him. After he arrived, we went on a fairy-tale vacation to Florida, where we swam with dolphins and saw Sea World˚. This was a first in the lives of the children. I never had the money for the extravagance of fun trips. It was like living inside a fantasy world, and we didn't want it to end. We shared much laughter and fun during that week, but the return to real life was far from being a fantasy world. Six months apart had been difficult for me because I returned to a former way of life filled with handling responsibility from a deep well of loneliness. But John had traveled down a different road. He had not returned to the old way of doing things. In fact, he had carried out missions that made him a new and different man. He still loved me and showed that, but he had to cope with trying to live a normal life in a world that would never seem ordinary to him again. Memories that he couldn't share would spontaneously come to his mind in the middle of his now ordinary days. The only place that made any sense to him, indeed, the only place that was safe for him anymore was the strictly ordered world of the military. Every aspect of his life was handled within a stringent chain of command.

John was now fully and completely a soldier and we became his troops. As teenagers, the children pushed back against the barked orders. As a formerly abused woman who had been serving as head of the household, I shrank back from him, confused by who he had become. Finally, one day, my flight or fight reflex took over, and this time, I chose to fight over flight. I fought for my marriage, not against my husband. With a new found determination stemming from the knowledge that I had something real that was worth fighting for, I sat my husband down and firmly explained to him that we were his family, not his soldiers or subordinates. His time at home between deployments became calmer, but then all too soon, he deployed to the Middle East again.

Our life settled into a pattern that is common to military families. We learned how to be together as a family while John was stateside, and we would adjust to the times when he was deployed halfway around the world. The connection within the military community was an essential part of my life. That allowed the kids and me to keep busy and to ward off some of the loneliness while John was gone. It was also the core of our social life when he was home. During one of the times of a social get-together after his second deployment, the reality of what his "job" really entailed was accidentally revealed to me.

We had a group of friends over for a party, and one of his team members loaded some of the pictures he had taken during their latest mission onto our laptop to share with the other guys. I stepped into the room, unprepared for what I would find there. As I looked at the images right in front of me, I knew there was no way I would be able to keep denying the reality of war in John's life. He was in a battle every day. A battle against evil, a battle for freedom for an oppressed group of people, a battle for his own life, a battle that required un-imaginable acts of courage to ensure he lived. My party mood left me at that moment, and the gravity of his "job" never left my mind from then on.

Blending two families into one is a monumental job in the very best of circumstances. Accomplishing it in the midst of the cycle of times of deployment and then a return to the base during the first two years of marriage is certainly not the best of circumstances. When you factor in teenager issues, it becomes difficult at best and impossible at worst. When John deployed the third time, Mason began acting out in extreme ways. His sadness over John leaving and then his rebellion to John's authority upon his return became our roller-coaster way of life. It soon became apparent that Mason was trying to follow in John's footsteps. But rather than choosing the path of the strong, mighty man he had become, he was drawn to the ways of John's teenage years. John was in Iraq fighting to win freedom against evil, and Mason was fighting me to win his freedom to experience evil things. He was smoking cigarettes and marijuana, breaking into houses, and becoming harder and harder for me to handle. He joined in gang activity, and I was desperate to help him get back on track, but at fourteen, he was strong-willed and determined to follow the wrong path. The "last straw" came when he broke into my neighbor's house, and I went to the neighbor and pleaded for my son. *"Please."* I begged, *"Please call the police and press charges!"* A mother's heart always wants what is best for her child, and at this very moment, I knew my son needed to experience the consequences of the choices he was making in a way that would help him choose something different. Sitting on the curb, watching the police car pull away, my flowing tears were bitter, and my heart was broken. Tia, as devastated as I was, sat with me that dark night, and I attempted to explain to her that it was the only way to get her brother help. I wanted to give her hope. I also wanted to find some for myself. Later that year, Mason and John came back home about the same time. Very soon, it was apparent that they could not get along.

As a last resort, Mason was sent to a boy's home for a year. As hard as that separation was, we all were grateful when we saw it brought the help he needed, and he began to straighten out. John knew the road Mason had tried to travel and continued to enforce rules meant to protect him. The tension in our family was still intense, the hurt feelings still raw, we couldn't find a way to bridge the difference of opinions that divided us.

Mason and Tia decided to go live with their father, and their decision shattered what was left of the shred of hope I had in my mother's heart. John was stationed state-side, but now his highly classified top secret job required that he be gone Monday through Friday. My lonely despair came back stronger than ever and filled my life where my family had once been. Alcohol became my way of getting through the silent nights lived out in my empty house. It is a powerful and cunning drug. It seems to lift the pain while, in fact, it pulls you ever more deeply into it. It brought me so far down into the darkness that several times, I again attempted to end my life. An ancient wise man, Erasmus, once said, "Bidden or unbidden God is present." I still had not come to know God, and yet I look back now and realize he was sending me help. We were invited to attend the church of a friend, and even as broken as we both were, we began to go. The people we met there welcomed us and included us in their family. At first, our lives didn't change much, and we partied with our friends on weekends but then went to church on Sunday. It became a place where we worshipped, served, and began to hear about a God who wanted to make our lives different. We heard He wanted a relationship with us.

Ft. Bragg Family Support
John's Story

The Fort Bragg family support group kept Angel, and the other wives informed about when we would return from Iraq, so she knew the date that we were going to land.

Arriving home, there was a real problem with me reintegrating with my family and other civilians. Angel and the kids never knew which John would walk through the door; the hard-core Green Beret or a loving husband and father. Angel later said that whenever I returned back from a deployment, I always seemed extremely angry. At the time, I was drinking a lot, and I think most of my poor behavior was because of the alcohol I was consuming. I never wanted it to happen, but my family became frightened of me. They had heard several stories about Green Berets "snapping" and harming or killing their wives and children, and my actions and angry demeanor did nothing to reassure them that they were safe with me.

Angel's Brother and Parents Die
Her Story

One day I finished a twelve-hour shift wholly exhausted. My job at the post office was hard work done in a harsh environment. At the end of days like this one, I questioned my decision to leave my twenty-year career as a CNA, certified nursing assistant. That job allowed me to help patients or clients with healthcare needs under the supervision of a Registered Nurse (RN) or a Licensed Practical Nurse (LPN).) But even with all my work to get my associate's nursing degree, I had eventually burned out caring for others. For now, the post office job provided income, but I realized it cost me time with my husband, whose state-side work schedule was different from mine. Entering our home, I was surprised to find John there and glad to have a little time with him before heading off to bed.

I quickly fell into a deep sleep that ended after only a short time when John gently shook me awake and asked me to come into the living room because he needed to tell me something. As I sat next to him on the sofa, he said that my sister had just called and told him that my brother had been shot in a hunting accident and had died. I heard John's words, but their meaning seemed impossible. It made no sense, and there was no reality behind them for me. We had all been raised knowing how to safely handle guns. This must just be a dream. After crying on John's shoulder as he comforted me for a while, I went back to bed and slept until my alarm woke me for my next workday. I had an important test scheduled for a job evaluation, so I drove to the testing site. En route, I realized it was true. My brother was dead! Unstoppable tears began to flow, but I put on sunglasses and went in to take the test. After a short time, the supervisor realized I was having a problem, and upon questioning me, sent me home. John helped me make travel plans, and somehow I moved through the following sur-real days. The facts about the shooting seemed impossible. Memories came flooding into my mind about spending time with my father.

One day when I was sixteen, my dad came home and told me to pack some clothes and go with him. Deep inside, I had a secret desire that finally he was done with his marriage to my mother. I thought, *"Now he is leaving her, and he's taking me with him."* As we drove that day, it became apparent that I was mistaken. We were going to his cabin in the Michigan woods. We were going to the very place he went to often, leaving me behind to endure my mother's wrath. My dad saw this trip as my rite of passage. The weekend was filled with the simple pleasures that were found there in the beautiful Michigan forest. It was also when he taught me how to handle guns. He taught me to respect them, to always be careful as I handled them, and he showed me how to shoot at targets. It was an enormous responsibility, and he was showing me that he knew I was ready to handle it. The simple cabin had no kitchen, and as our food cooked over the open flames of the campfire the last night of our stay, a deep sense of understanding filled my heart. In that place, I felt a peace I had never experienced anywhere else. With no discussion between us, I came to understand that this was where he went when he reached a breaking point in his marriage. It was never that he was deliberately leaving me behind to endure my mother's wrath as I initially thought; he was just trying to save himself.

My dad had spent many hours with my brothers on other weekend trips to the cabin. He had taught them the same respect and responsibility for handling guns. He had also instilled in them his love for the outdoors. It became a deep heart-connection between them and a lifelong activity they shared. For the past five years, my brother had been inviting my father to go with him on his annual deer hunting trip to North Dakota. Finally, Dad agreed to go. There was much happy anticipation about sharing the journey. My brother bought a new truck, and they both bought new rifles. They had scouted the area and finally were ready to hunt. Then as my father laid his loaded gun down in the bed of the pickup, it unexpectedly discharged—just as my brother walked past the back of the truck. The bullet struck him in the side. My brother's last and only words uttered that day were simply, "I'm hit."

The powerful impact of those words on my dad was unimaginable. His actions and his rifle had taken away his son, who was his best friend and who shared his love for the outdoors. He was gone in a split second. My brother died with his head in my father's lap as they unsuccessfully tried to get him to a hospital in time to save his life.

My first concern was about how my father could possibly get through this loss. When he returned home, his response surprised me because the first thing he said to John was, "I need prayers." This was the first time he had ever spoken about God or Jesus, and he had never before asked for prayers. My amazement continued when my sister-in-law told us that ten days before the hunting trip, my brother had accepted the Lord as Savior and had been baptized. John used this as an opportunity to reach out to my father and said, "If your son believed in Christ, don't you think it is important for you to believe also?" Those words pierced my father's heart and brought him to a personal relationship with Jesus that day. I watched as God sustained him through the process of saying good-bye to this good son of his in the aftermath of a horrible tragedy. After the funeral, as I sat with him, I asked, "Dad, how are you feeling?" His response relieved my concern when he said, "I don't feel any sadness or pain because Jesus took it all away from me." Those words were said with the calm assurance of someone who truly knows the Lord.

Over the next several months, our family grieved over not having my brother with us anymore, but we mourned with new hope because we all became aware of the presence of Jesus in our lives. My mother professed her faith in the Lord, and I did as well. I thought in the first moments of my new life, *"Jesus, now I see how You have been there all along in my life, and I fully surrender to You. I give my life to You."*

On December 31ˢᵗ, both of my parents and I were baptized by my husband, John. The Scriptures tell us that God will turn everything into good for those who love Him. As my brother came to love God, the Lord then turned this tragic end of his life into the amazing good of seeing his earthly family become his eternal family.

Once my mother became a Christian, she changed. Since I was now married to John, she began to see me as less of a threat, knowing that I would not be running back home to my dad. Over time, we were able to mend our relationship. She actually came to me and said she was sorry for the things she had done and apologized for being the kind of mother she had been to me. I also apologized for my part of the anger and the things I had done to her. We were finally at a place of peace with one another. She began to tell me she loved me every time I left one of our visits, and I began to believe her.

God knows everything from the beginning to the end. We believe the death of my brother brought about the salvation of my father at a crucial time in his life. From the time he was saved after my brother's death, he began to read the Bible every day. Then only a year after my brother's death, Dad was diagnosed with cancer. It was a difficult journey, but through his faith and medical treatments, he went into remission for a short time, but then the cancer returned. When John learned we were going to be stationed in Texas, I decided to go home for a visit because Dad's cancer had worsened, and we were told that it now was terminal. In a fall, my mother had recently broken her hip, so she was living in a long-term rehabilitation facility. I obtained a power of attorney for her care because I didn't want to leave her alone in Michigan in a nursing home and was planning to take her to Texas with us. However, before that move happened, she had a sudden and unexpected brain aneurysm and died. My suffering father was barely able to attend her funeral, and it was an emotional moment when, with all the strength he had left, he went forward to her casket and shakily standing there, touched her one last time to say his good-bye. My mother's body had always been very emaciated by the excessive amounts of alcohol she drank. However, since she couldn't drink during rehab, she had gained some weight, and my dad later said how beautiful she was and how she looked like she had been when she was in her thirties as a young woman. That was the image of her he held in his heart. He had never given up the hope of seeing her like that again, even when she had been overcome by alcohol. I was grateful they had shared an undeniable love, and I finally understood why he never left her.

Dad took her death very hard, and his health declined rapidly. One day, while we were at home, he looked at me, and weakly said, "It's time." The nurses came, and he was taken to a hospice facility. It was difficult for me to let them take him, but I quickly got ready and went there to be with him. Once I arrived, I was astonished because this place was a cabin. His room had French doors that opened up, allowing his bed to be rolled onto an outside porch. He was surrounded by nature and the woods he so loved and where he had found refuge that sustained him as he dealt with the chaos of his marriage. It was a beautiful place for him to have his last experience on earth. And now that I knew he was a believer, I understood it was also a preview of the beauty and peace he would soon have forever as he joined his son and wife in heaven.

John Deploys to Afghanistan

Angel At Deployment Drive

John With Mason and Tia

John Baptizes Angel, Sylvia, and Robert

Angel with Robert and Sylvia

✝✝✝

CHAPTER FOUR

Fort Bragg & Downrange

On June 1, 2004, I signed into the 3rd Special Forces Group (A), which is on Fort Bragg, North Carolina. I had just finished Army SERE School, which was an acronym for Survival Evasion Resistance and Escape. The third Special Forces group was divided into three battalions; first, second, and third battalions. I was assigned to the second battalion. When I arrived there, they were getting ready to deploy to an area of operation (AO) in Afghanistan, working out of Bagram Airfield. I met with the unit Sergeant Major who said, "John, you will meet us in Afghanistan in fifteen days, so get your family situated because we're going to kill as many bad guys as we possibly can." As a young staff sergeant, I remembered the goosebumps on my arms and spine as I thought, "This is exactly why I joined Special Forces not only to kill bad people but to rid the world from the evildoers by going behind enemy lines and on clandestine missions to prevent them from harming others."

Fifteen days passed by quickly, and I boarded a Boeing C-17 Globemaster III at Pope Air Force Base. The inside of the aircraft was gigantic! Amazingly, they can land on small runways as short as 3,500 feet and can perform a three-point turn using reverse thrusters to turn around on runways as narrow as ninety feet wide. They carry one hundred and two combat-ready troops plus 170,900 pounds of cargo. *(A C-17 aircraft travels along with the President's plane, Air Force One, transporting both the President's limousines and the security detachments when the President makes visits within the United States and at foreign locations around the globe.)*

We arrived at Ramstein Air Base near the city of Frankfurt, Germany. The aircraft was refueled, then after a ten-hour break, we took off and flew to Afghanistan landing at Kandahar in the early evening. Stepping off the airplane, the first thing I noticed was an incredible 100° heat wave that blasted me in the face. I thought, *"Wow, we really are in the desert."* Having never been in a combat environment before, I remember thinking, *"This is unreal. It looks like a scene out of a Hollywood movie."* Dust was blowing everywhere and getting in my eyes and mouth. Soldiers were walking and running around carrying weapons. Fully armored Humvees and trucks were driving inside the compound perimeter. It was a beehive of activity, and I was excited to finally be here. In the distance, I saw many high mountaintops, and for a Southern California guy, I was amazed.

I was taken to 3rd Battalion 3rd Special Forces headquarters, which was just being set up. We stayed there overnight in temporary quarters and then because I was with 2nd Battalion 3rd Special Forces, the next day I was taken to Bagram Air Force Base. At four thousand seven hundred feet, it is situated in a broad valley and is the largest United States military complex in Afghanistan. Located fifteen miles north of the capital Kabul, the base is hemmed in by tall mountains to the northeast, which are part of the Eastern Hindu Kush range of the Himalayas.

It was a massive facility with two long runways capable of handling the biggest aircraft in the world. The perimeter contained tall fencing with massive amounts of razor-sharp concertina wire attached and guard towers strategically placed to provide interlocking fields of machinegun fire. Inside were numerous permanent and semi-permanent structures built by Kellogg, Brown and Root (KBR). The amount of equipment, vehicles, trucks, Humvees, and other things was staggering.

Hesco structures were built everywhere. They were tall, large wire wrapped nylon structures which were filled with sand and used as walls that surrounded various compounds within the perimeter of the base. They served two purposes. First acting as blast barriers in the event of enemy incoming mortar and rocket fire and secondly to prevent anyone from observing the activities within the compound.

At headquarters, I met the 2rd Battalion 3rd Special Forces Sergeant Major, who sat me down and said, "I haven't got you assigned to an Operational Detachment Alpha (ODA) yet but give me a few days and I will. Go with the supply sergeant, and he will set you up with all the gear that you need and will find a place for you to sleep for the next few days until you finally meet up with your ODA." Standing up, I said, "Yes, Sergeant Major. I appreciate all your help and look forward to being in the unit where you place me."

I was taken to Special Forces Camp Vance and stayed there a week until I received orders for my new unit. Camp Vance was named after Staff Sergeant Gene Arden Vance, of the 19th Special Forces Group, who was killed in action on May 19, 2002, during Operation Enduring Freedom. After about a week, the Sergeant Major came to me and said, "You're going to be assigned to ODA 342 (3rd Special Forces Group, 4th company, 2nd team) in Gardez about a three and one-half hours' drive from here."

Gardez, located in the highlands of the Hindu Kush Mountains, is seven thousand five hundred seventy-two feet above sea level, making it the third-highest provincial capital in Afghanistan, and is not far from Tora Bora *(Pashto: Black Caves)* near the Pakistan border. It is a vast region of caves and tunnels where Osama Bin Laden previously was headquartered and hiding.

Before I left the Sergeant Major's office, he said, "You'll be flying on a CH-47 Chinook resupply helicopter "Ring" flight that will take you there." I asked, "Where can I get a weapon?" He said, "You won't get a weapon until you arrive at your new unit in Gardez." Surprised, I said, "So I'm going to be leaving a secure base flying to a combat location, and I won't have any type of weapon to protect myself if we go down. Is that what you're saying, Sergeant Major?" Leaning back is in his chair he smiled and said, "Son, that's the nature of the beast. But you'll be okay."

The next day I got on the Chinook and sat down, stacking my gear on either side of me on the fold-down nylon seats attached to the walls. Across from me were two guys with precisely the same equipment and looked like either Navy SEALs or Green Berets because of their long hair under baseball caps and full beards. "Are you guys Navy SEALs?" I asked. "No. We're Special Forces." Then they shut up. After making several other stops, we landed at Gardez, and I walked down the rear ramp. Standing there, I looked around, wondering if somebody would come up to me and welcome me to the unit; however, no one did. Then someone drove up on a four-wheeler ATV carrying a weapon across his back wearing shorts, a full beard, and long hair under a baseball cap. I walked up to him and asked, "Are you with ODA 342?" "Yes, I am. Who are you?" He asked. "I'm the new eighteen bravo assigned to the unit," I answered. "No one is expecting a new guy but load your gear on the back, and I'll take you to the headquarters compound." Arriving there, I met the team leader and the team sergeant. I also was finally issued weapons and assigned living quarters.

My first mission in the field was a "presence patrol," which was basically a meet and greet of the local tribal leaders and village elders in remote locations in the mountains. Many times we had intelligence briefings that directed us into a particular area, and other times we traveled to villages with no idea what to expect or what the reception was going to be. Usually, we traveled forty to fifty kilometers (approximately twenty-five to thirty-one miles) away from Gardez to these small communities.

Virtually everywhere we went was on the dirt roads, and we traveled in small convoys of three lightly armored Humvees with the doors removed so that we could exit them quickly if we got in a firefight. In 2004, improvised explosive devices (IEDs) were not a real problem, so we really didn't have to worry about them as we traveled the dusty roads to the remote villages. However, in 2006 and 2007, they were adopted by the Taliban and Al Qaeda from the terrorists in Iraq, and IEDs became a favorite method of killing Americans, NATO forces, and the Afghanistan Army soldiers.

The right door was removed from the Humvee, and a swing arm had been attached to the door frame. This served as the movable mount for the M-240 machine gun, which fired a 7.62mm NATO round. Attached to the weapon was an ammo can containing two hundred rounds of metal linked ammo. A Browning M-2 .50 caliber machine gun was mounted on a revolving turret on top of the vehicle. Instead of a machine gun, one vehicle was equipped with a top-mounted Mark-19, belt-fed 40 mm grenade launcher, which was capable of firing sixty hand grenades per minute. So when we traveled, we were heavily armed. We went with all that firepower and our individually issued M-4 rifles in 5.56 mm caliber and Beretta M-9's in 9 mm Parabellum.

All of the small villages looked alike with mud and straw huts and flat roofs with some cattle, sheep, and goats inside their walled closures. The people were extremely wary of our presence and usually only stared or glared at us as we slowly drove by them. Occasionally the villages had electricity, and frequently the wires were hung very low from rooftop to rooftop, so we learned very quickly to lower our antennas down and attach them to straps at the front of Humvee, so we didn't knock the wires down as we passed under.

On one occasion, I failed to lower my antenna as we entered a village, and I started knocking down power lines. Suddenly the intelligence sergeant came running up to me yelling at me to drop the antenna because I was destroying all of his goodwill he had established with the villagers.

Each of the villages had its own small police force generally located in the center so frequently we saw an Afghani policeman walking around carrying an AK-47, which always made me very uncomfortable. There were many times when we rolled through villages, and as I looked at some people, I knew that they were the "evil ones" who would be shooting at us in the future.

At the base, an Afghan security force led by commander "G" provided all of our security and sometimes would go with us on specific missions into remote areas of the country. He and his militiamen lived outside the perimeter of Gardez but from time to time, worked inside. However, every day at 1800 hours, they were required to leave the compound.

One of my jobs as the 18 Bravo (weapons sergeant) was to ensure that we had a forward operating base (FOB) defense plan and that all the Americans located in nearby encampments knew their role to ensure they would correctly implement it if we were under attack. That included several civilian Blackwater and DynCorp special operators living approximately two miles from our location, who generally trained the Afghanistan police forces. They also were responsible for threat assessment protection, perimeter security, base security, and guard services. DynCorp supported the U.S. Army with vehicle searches, roving patrols, and explosive-detecting dogs and provided personal protection for high ranking politicians who visited many regions of Iraq and Afghanistan.

One of our main programs was to buy back arms and ammunition brought to us by Afghani's. We paid American dollars to anyone who brought us weapons or led us to caches of munitions, which we would then blow up. Many times we had large truckloads of arms and ammunition brought to us, and the way we looked at it was everything turned into us probably saved the life of an American or allied soldier. We purchased Russian-made landmines, 105 mm recoilless rifles, RPG-2's, RPG-7's, and other exotic weapons and explosives.

Frequently we received intelligence reports asking us to capture or kill a "high-value" individual that had been discovered living in our area of operations (AO). These were called "snatch and grab" missions. So in addition to our building indigenous personnel relationships through our "hearts and minds" programs and civil affairs med-cap programs (where we took doctors, medics and dentist into the villages and provided free medical care, medicine, and dental work to Afghanistan people who were ill or injured) we hunted down specific enemy targets.

Our interpreters said the villagers called us the "bearded ones" because we had a reputation of standing and fighting if attacked, and the word on the street was to let us go by and not engage us at all. But on one occasion, two Green Berets were killed in a sister company ODA in the Gharbi Mangretay Valley, so a companywide mission was planned. It started when we heard in the radio room the words *"Troops in contact! Troops in contact!* Once that was said, then everybody in the field maintained radio silence, so the frequencies were free of any unnecessary talking or chatter, and everyone was focused on the people in a firefight.

The battalion commander, a lieutenant colonel, came into the radio room, took the microphone, and said, "Status report?" The immediate response was, "Two individuals are being manually resuscitated." Which meant that two Green Berets had been shot by snipers and were down. The term "killed in action" (KIA) was never used over the radios because until a physician confirmed the status, we could only say the person was being "manually resuscitated." After flying the two individuals out of the valley by helicopter, the ODA was taken to Bagram Airfield, and after a ceremony, the two bodies were returned to the United States.

Because the detachment-size ODA element had lost two members, they were given time to recover; however, one morning before sunrise, five ODA's landed in the valley where the two Green Berets had been killed. We were told to expect a firefight as soon as we offloaded from the helicopters. Cobra gunships were used to escort our helicopters and to provide air support if we began to receive small arms fire. Suddenly over the radio, someone whispered, "They know we are here, so get ready." But as the sun rose above the mountains, none of the enemy combatants engaged us. The ODA that lost the two team members attached the biggest American flag they could find to a vehicle with a tall radio antenna and slowly drove through the valley where they had lost their brothers. As the Humvee passed by me, I looked at the soldier standing in the turret, we locked eyes, and I gave him a thumbs-up, and he returned it back to me.

Once the solitary flag-waving Humvee had slowly passed through the village all of the support aircraft, U.S. Army Cobras and Apache gunships, began to systematically fire their rockets and machine guns destroying every structure, building, hut, and house until nothing was left standing but a smoking pile of rubble that had been the village. After everything was leveled in the valley, all was eerily quiet, and the Chinooks came in and landed. All of the ODA's were loaded and returned to their respective FOBs. The lesson the enemy learned that day was to never mess with Green Berets, or else you will suffer the devastating consequences!

Sometime later, we received an intelligence briefing indicating that a force of Taliban and Al Qaeda fighters were gathering at a checkpoint near the Pakistani border not far from us. Meeting the police force at the checkpoint, we decided to demonstrate to the bad guys and the surrounding enemy combatants in the hills what an American "show of force" looked like. All of the vehicles were placed side by side on the dirt road leading up to the nearby border crossing; then at the command "Fire" everyone began firing their weapons including the .50 caliber turret-mounted machine guns, M-19 belt-fed grenade launcher, M-240, 7.62 mm machine gun and our personal side arms. The sound was earsplitting, and the firepower was massive from all of the ordinance being expended.

Later that afternoon, with an Air Force combat controller, we climbed to the top of a nearby mountain and set up a remain overnight (RON) perimeter. At midnight we began receiving mortar fire from all around us. The combat controller called in a USAF F-16 fighter who arrived in just a few minutes. Circling overhead, he called down to us and said he could see where the rounds were coming from but could not tell who was firing at us. Then the ground controller pulled out a device that was basically a high-intensity laser flashlight that could actually blind you if it shined in your eyes. With it on, he began to move it in a circular motion, which he called "Roping us in." The F-16 pilot immediately got on the radio and said, "I can clearly see you now." Suddenly, all of the mortars stopped at the same time, and everything was quiet except for the sound of the "fast mover" circling above. We never learned who was firing at us, but clearly, they were trying to bracket our location and drop mortars on our position. I realized then how important it was for us to maintain air superiority and how the power of the United States military kept us safe no matter where we were located. It was a lesson I never forgot and appreciated for the remainder of my tours in Afghanistan and Iraq.

Just before my rotation ended, my team sergeant came to me one day and said, "We've got several new guys that just came in, and with you, I'm going to take them out on a five-day dismounted patrol to "confirm and deny" enemy routes. We will be climbing from 8,000 feet to 12,000 feet and back down to 8,000 feet. I asked him, "Why are you only going to take the new guys and me with you?" He laughingly responded, "Because when you are new, you always remember the "shit" missions." We spent five days climbing with all of our gear and heavy packs up and down mountains, and all we confirmed was that a lot of cow manure, sheep, and goat droppings were on the ground. But he was absolutely right because I've never forgotten that particular mission.

One day, while I was sitting in the radio room, a call came in saying, *"Troops in contact! Troops in contact! Maintain radio silence!"* That was the time that a small group of Navy SEALs was attacked, and everyone was killed except Marcus Luttrell. The Hollywood movie *"Lone Survivor"* with actor Mark Wahlberg is the story of that mission. A coordinated rescue effort was immediately started that included U.S. Army Rangers, regular Army soldiers, Navy SEALs, and Green Berets to find him. An ODA in Charlie Company was the one that actually found and rescued him in the Afghanistan village where he was being held.

A few weeks later, our battalion commander came to us and said, "With the war shutting down, we are going to pack things up and shift our focus to other areas and then ultimately move into Iraq. You guys are going to close down Gardez and move into Mazar-i-Sharif and Kunduz. ODA 342 you will be the first detachment to go back into the North where the 5th Special Forces first entered Afghanistan on horseback with the Northern Alliance when the war started in

2001. To get there, you will have to go over the Hindu Kush mountain passes, and because of their altitude, you will not have any helicopter escorts or gunships because they can't fly that high. So you will be completely on your own for a while."

We got to Mazar-i-Sharif without incident but had to stay at a German military compound until we built our own. They were very upset that we were staying with them because they felt that our presence was going to make them a target of the Taliban and Al Qaeda. They told us, "If any of you guys get hurt, we are not going to assist you nor share our blood with you, so you are on your own." While there, fortunately, none of us were seriously injured nor wounded, and we did not have to see if they really meant what they had said.

John's Faith

Before my first deployment to Afghanistan, my grandmother "Rosie," a devout Catholic, gave me a small bottle of anointing oil. She was a dedicated believer of Jesus and a mighty prayer warrior and told me, "Mijo (Spanish: My Son) As you plead the blood of Jesus over all the equipment, facilities, and personal gear, place a small drop of this on it for protection." I had gone to church on all of the major holidays like Christmas and Easter and had a lukewarm relationship with Jesus, but frankly, I had more faith in my grandmother and her beliefs. So, before we left our forward operating base (FOB) and the safety of its concertina wire encircled interior, to go out on combat patrols, I went to each vehicle with my anointing oil and placed a small cross of it on the center of the steering wheel which the driver would be touching. Then I put a small drop on the hood of the vehicle and made a small cross. I did that with all of the Humvees and equipment carriers that we used on missions, praying that we would all be safe outside the wire.

After three months of anointing everything that we used on a mission a "Junior Charlie" who was the explosives engineer came to me and said, "John, I know that you anoint our equipment and gear and we really appreciate you doing that; however, can you please stop it for a while. We're Green Berets, and we want to get into contact with the enemy, and your prayers and anointing everything are protecting us." The senior communications specialist who was standing next to me incredulously looked at him and said, "Why in the world would you ask him to stop praying just so we can start getting shot at?" So, I continued to anoint everything, and I am convinced that the anointing oil my grandmother gave me protected everyone in my unit.

The Meat-Eaters Pool

Several months after returning home to Fort Bragg, Company B, 2nd Battalion, 3rd Special Forces was scheduled for a six-month rotation to Iraq in July 2007; however, I was sent to another school called the Special Forces assaulters' school. The full name was "Special Forces Advanced Reconnaissance, Target Analysis & Target Exploitation Techniques Course (SFARTAETC). Basically, it trained Green Berets in tactical breaching techniques for buildings, structures, and houses to quickly enter and either capture or kill enemy combatants. To begin the course, I had to "shoot my way in." In other words, I had to qualify with my Beretta M-9 pistol utilizing various positions, i.e., standing upright, squatting, and lying down prone while shooting at a target twenty-five yards away. My scores were below the minimum required, and I did not get into SFARTAETC.

Nobody expects to fail, nor do they like it if it happens. I was no different. I felt like a failure. It was a very humbling experience for me to go back to my unit and confront all of the type "A" personalities and "meat-eaters" there. However, I was accepted back with no problem, and the Sergeant Major said that I could attend the course after I returned from Iraq, but for the time being, they needed me as part of the team. I was very grateful for their acceptance and compassion in this situation.

In September 2007, I arrived in Baghdad, Iraq, at Camp Liberty. The base was a large coalition military installation located northeast of the Baghdad International Airport and was part of the U.S. military's Victory Base Complex. It also was one of the largest United States overseas posts built since the Vietnam War. Inside the base were US Special Forces, Army Rangers, Delta Force and British SAS all involved in clandestine missions.

One night after settling in with my unit, I went out with my team and was carrying an M-72 LAW, which is an acronym for a Light Antitank Weapon. It was a short shoulder-fired solid rocket propulsion device that launched a sixty-six-millimeter high explosive warhead against a target. This night I was with a cell that had been inserted into a remote area by helicopters landing approximately two kilometers away from a house that intelligence had determined contained a high-value target (HVT). Our cell met up with two others, and in an "L" shape assault formation, we approached the large front wooden door of the compound. As we got closer to it, we begin receiving small arms fire.

Suddenly the ISR (Intelligence, Surveillance, and Reconnaissance) aircraft flying above, which provided a live video feed of everything on the ground, called us and said, "Stop moving! There's an enemy fighter crawling on the ground to your location, and you can't see him because he's in the tall grass. So, we are going to "sparkle" him." Then from high above us, a laser beam which only we could see through our night vision goggles began shining down from a circling stealth aircraft and pinpointed the enemy combatant's head.

Slowly and quietly backing away a safe distance, two members of the cell tossed hand grenades onto him and took him out. Then the cell leader softly called me up to the front of the formation and whispered, "John, I need you to blow open the wooden door to the compound with your LAW." Kneeling I extended the launch tube and placed it on my shoulder then my training kicked in, and I remembered to look behind me to make sure no one was in the back blast area. Turning my head around from the pop-up sights, I saw our unit dog handler with his canine on a leash four feet directly behind me. I called out, saying, "Back blast area, all clear!" Instantly, he dropped down and quickly pulled the dog away from the deadly area. I pressed down on the trigger, and the explosive projectile shot out of the tube and hit the side of a white van parked beside the door entrance, ricocheted off, and struck the wooden door dead center. It blew up with a massive explosion and set off a secondary blast inside the house. Then the van began to burn, and because it was filled with explosives and ammunition, everything began to "cook-off" and blow up. By now, more enemy fighters began maneuvering towards us, so the team leaders decided it was time to call in the Air Force's "fast movers" and drop JDAM's on the entire compound.

JDAM's are Joint Direct Attack Munitions, which basically are 2,000 pound "dumb" bombs attached to a GPS guidance system with moveable fins that flies it into a specific target location designated by its longitude and latitude. Dropped at 30,000 feet and fifteen miles away, they are accurate to within thirteen meters from the center of the target area. We immediately withdrew a safe distance from the compound and watched as the GPU-31's pulverized everything and everyone inside the high walled camp.

Lying on the ground to minimize the effects of the bomb concussion waves, we began receiving AK-47 small arms fire from a house behind us. Hugging the ground as low as possible, I thought about my wife, *I wonder if Angel knows what I'm doing right now? What is she doing? Are the kids getting ready for school? Does she know that her husband's in a fight for his life? Is she on aisle seven at Wal-Mart buying cereal?* I began to think about all the things that I had not done with my family and regretted not spending more time with them. Then as several bullets "popped" close by my head, I quickly put the thoughts of home aside. Suddenly the enemy combatants stopped shooting at us probably because they saw the large compound being leveled and obliterated by the JDAM's and didn't want the same to happen to them.

Returning back to the site after the bombs had destroyed the compound, the dog handler and his German shepherd started finding several enemy insurgents still lying in the grass. After locating the first one, the dog was shot and killed by a second guy hiding in the grass. The man was immediately killed by other Green Berets. But we knew for sure that the combination of the "sparkle" and the dog had saved some of our lives. At daylight, helicopters came in and extracted us, and we flew back to Camp Liberty.

We continued to go out on more "door kicking" missions for several months, and then one evening, I heard someone yell, *"Cell Leaders!"* That was the signal for everyone to begin putting on their gear and gathering their weapons. After their briefing, the leaders came back telling us this was going to be a fun mission because we were going into our objective on boats. That night at 0100 hours, after all of us were loaded on several Blackhawk helicopters, we linked up with the Navy's premier Special Operations Boat Unit known as (SBUs) on the Euphrates River west of Baghdad. These boats had more fire-power than anything I had ever seen. Each one was equipped with a pintle-mounted 7.62 mm six-barrel mini-gun. A Browning M-2 .50

caliber heavy machine gun and Twin M-240, 7.62 mm machine guns were mounted front and rear.

Quietly going up the river, we approached the target house and silently glided to the river bank. Our mission was to capture a high ranking civilian. Disembarking from the boats, we got into our familiar "L" formation and approached the front door. One of the lead guys pulled the pin on an M-84 stun grenade and threw it in the open front door. The explosion was deafening and was intended to cause disorientation of the people inside the house. Immediately the interpreters started yelling a "Call Out" in Arabic, which basically was for the inhabitants to surrender immediately. We captured our guy and covered his head with a black cloth and brought him back to the SBU where he and the team were loaded, and we all returned to our departure point on the Euphrates River. Before leaving the house, we searched it and removed all the cell phones, laptops, computers, electronic devices, and anything else that would be of military intelligence value.

A few nights later, at Camp Liberty, I again heard someone loudly yell, *"Cell Leaders,"* and I began to put on all my gear, making sure I had my basic load of ammunition. Then we loaded on three Blackhawk helicopters and left. There was a heavy nylon strap attached to the aircraft door facing that kept us from falling out, and we also had a lanyard on our belt, which we attached to a "D" ring on the helicopter cargo floor. As we were flying away from Baghdad and our base, I remember thinking as I sat with my feet dangling out the open door, "Iraq is beautiful with all of the tall palm trees, green fields, waterways, and even the moonlit desert landscape. I can't believe we are in a war zone that looks a lot like South Florida.

Suddenly I began to see several large balls of light going past the aircraft and watched them in fascination. Turning to the crew chief sitting next to me, I yelled, "What was that?" The crew chief laughed and said, "We just flew through a friendly artillery fire mission!" It was then that I understood what the term "pucker factor" was all about.

Arriving at the farmhouse, we captured the bad guy, put a hood on his head, and then called in the helicopters to pick us up. All of my guys were huge special operators with all their gear and guns, so there wasn't a whole lot of room to sit on the back cargo floor. Just as I climbed aboard, the crew chief yelled, "Hook up, guys, we're taking off." I was still standing on the right skid and not sitting down because there was no room for me. As the aircraft lifted off, immediately, we were enveloped in a brownout of dust and sand. I started frantically yelling, "I'm not on! I'm not on!" But no one could hear me because of the sound of the rotor blades. The pilot made a hard right turn heading back to our base, and I was looking straight down at the ground, only holding on to the troop strap but not hooked up to the "D" ring. The only thing that kept me from falling out of the helicopter was the centrifugal force of the tight turn. Earlier in the year, several soldiers had died being inserted into an AO when the troop strap was unhooked, and they fell out of the helicopter. I believe that night; God protected me and kept me safe inside the cargo bay of the aircraft.

On December 1, 2007, we left Iraq and returned to Fort Bragg, North Carolina. En route, we stopped at Maron, Spain, to refuel; however, the aircraft broke down. While it was being repaired, we were put up in temporary housing and given permission to go into town but had to return to the airfield early the next morning. Several buddies of mine and I rented a car, and we drove into the city and spent some time sightseeing, taking pictures, and then we went to a local bar. Although I'm Hispanic, I never really learned to speak Spanish, but one of my buddies, who was a Caucasian, had been a missionary in Mexico for many years before entering the military, so he spoke fluent Spanish. As we were walking around town, he could communicate easily with everyone, but I could not. In Southern California, I was known as a "coconut," meaning I was brown on the outside but white on the inside. The Spaniards we met were surprised that I could not speak Spanish while my Caucasian friend was fluent in their language.

When we came out of the bar at 11:00 pm to go back to the base, standing there were dozens of very young Spanish girls twelve to fifteen-years-old all lined up outside waiting for men to pick them up and take them to several nearby shabby hotel rooms. It really bothered me to see what the young girls were doing to survive. I went up to several of them and in my broken Spanish, tried to convince them that what they were doing was wrong, harmful, and dangerous. But of course, they wouldn't listen to me. I believe at that moment, my eyes were opened to see how vulnerable some people are, and God told me, *"John, you are going to save many children in your lifetime."*

Grizzly Hitch & Ranger School

One day at Fort Bragg, my unit Sergeant Major called me into his office and said, "John, an opportunity has just opened up that will benefit your career if you're interested in this particular job with a state-side project team. I've set up an interview for you with its leadership. It's called the "Grizzly Hitch" team. It's an exceptional unit and the only one of its kind in the world, so this is a unique opportunity for you if you choose to participate. There will be twelve individuals hand-selected for this team."

I interviewed with the team leaders, and they hired me on the spot. So I immediately was reassigned to the Alpha Company 1st Battalion 3rd Special Forces, which was under the command of U.S. Army Special Operations Command (USASOC).

Designated ODA team 315, we were assigned all of our missions from several government agencies. Tasked with overseeing the security for various military and civilian contractor sites, we ensured the safety of our homeland, including nuclear reactors, ammunitions factories, rocket launch sites, etc. The mission was to review and test the security procedures of critical infrastructure within the United States by attempting to surreptitiously breach their defenses. Each week for three years, I traveled to different locations around the country with the team doing this. Then because it was my time to leave the team, the leader came to me and asked me what I wanted to do next. I told him that I wanted to go to Army Ranger School at Fort Benning, Georgia. So in July 2010, I was sent there.

To graduate, you must pass a physical exam, which included a five-mile run, and of course, in the middle of summer, the heat and humidity are oppressive. I did all my push-ups and sit-ups with no problem and then began the five-mile run, which must be completed in less than forty minutes, which is an eight-minute mile. We started at 4:00 am in the morning to beat the heat, and I finished the five miles in thirty-six minutes, but as I walked alone trying to cool off, I started feeling strange, had a severe headache, was nauseous, and then began to have trouble standing up straight. I walked over to the medical vehicle and took a knee and explained that I felt completely exhausted. One of the nearby medics came up to me and said, "Ranger, you are really overheated and need to come with me." They put me in an ambulance and took me to the hospital and then took my core temperature *(I won't tell you where they stuck the thermometer, but I will say the sun never shines there.)* It was 104.7°, and I was suffering from severe heat exhaustion. I had to withdraw from Ranger school and returned to my unit at Fort Bragg, once again feeling like a failure.

Afghanistan Landscape

Dismount Patrol, Afghanistan

Afghanistan Village

Ready To Wake Up the Bad Guys—Iraq

Empty LAW After Mission—Iraq

John After Clearing Routes

John In Helicopter—Iraq

Destroying Ammo Cache—Afghanistan

Prepping For Big Boom—Afghanistan

Ammo Exploded

Afghan Camel Transport

Humvee Patrol

Confirming Enemy Routes

John With Afghan Kids

John With German Soldier

Pullups on a Russian Tank—Afghanistan

John Downrange

Resting During a Patrol

John in Afghanistan

John Taking Break on Patrol

Calling In Our Location

John With .50 caliber

Winning Hearts & Minds

John with Rifle & 40mm Launcher

Recovering Supply Truck After ambush

†††

CHAPTER FIVE

Green to Gold

Back at Fort Bragg, I wasn't sure what I was going to do next. Was I going to go back to Ranger school in a few months, once the weather cooled off? I began to think about my career and what my plans were after I took off the uniform. Fortunately, the ODA to which I was assigned worked with several civilian government agencies. Working alongside these agencies, I was given a glimpse of life after the military, and one thing stood out the most, I needed more education. I don't know what changed inside me, but I wasn't so enthusiastic about Ranger school anymore. I began to research the application process to become an Army warrant officer. Quite often, Special Forces soldiers who are looking to advance their careers will pursue becoming a warrant officer. They are highly specialized experts and trainers in their career field. But as I began my research into that, a friend of mine told me about a new program that had just opened up called the "Active Duty Green to Gold" program, which took senior NCOs and sent them to college to become commissioned officers. This program was for enlisted soldiers who wanted to pursue a career as an Army officer. In most instances, soldiers temporarily left the Army, completed their bachelor's degree, and returned as commissioned Army officers.

Active duty Green-to-Gold was a new term to me. With this program, enlisted soldiers remained on active duty and kept their current rank and pay, less any hazardous duty money they received. There was no break in service required. As I sat with the counselor, I couldn't believe what I was hearing. I asked several times, "Are you sure I'm qualified for the active-duty program?" My counselor told me that based upon my current college credits, I was just a few shy of meeting the requirements, but the board did not meet until April, and by that time, I could have everything I needed. I met with the counselor in September 2010, and the Green-to-Gold board met in April 2011 with results to be released by June. Becoming an Army officer was never something I had thought about because I didn't believe I was smart enough or qualified to be one.

As a truck driver, I thought I did pretty well; however, as a Green Beret, I was in a small pool among big fish, and I was below the average size. I'd like to tell you that I was the best Green Beret out there, but I wasn't. I didn't succeed at everything I attempted. In a community of alpha male personalities, everyone is striving to be the best. I had just returned from Ranger school, where I was sent home early, and now I'm going to try and become an officer? Once you receive your commission, you are not only expected to succeed at what you attempt but achieve it with the highest standard. That is what is expected of U.S. Army leaders.

My team sergeant at the time was expecting me to return to Ranger school in the fall, but I dropped a bombshell on him when I said, "I'm applying to active duty Green-to-Gold." If I remember correctly, his jaw dropped, and he said, "What?" I told him that if I become an officer, I will go to Ranger school then. Frankly, I don't think anyone thought I would be selected.

Have you ever prayed for something and didn't get it? Then a few months or years go by, and you think back and say, "Thank you, God, for not answering that prayer." We serve a God that loves us so much that He's willing to save us from ourselves! As a Green Beret, I wanted it all, but it seemed the more I tried, the less I accomplished. Failure is not good, nor is it fun, but when it's divinely appointed, it causes you to humble yourself when you have succeeded. In dealing with others that have experienced failures, you will have a deeper understanding because you've been there.

I obtained all the course credits I needed and letters of recommendation from my senior leaders, and then it was time to submit my application. A few months went by, and finally, I received notification that I had been selected. Hallelujah! There was no time to wait. I was going to be a full-time college student again, and I was scared! I started questioning whether I was capable of succeeding at college. I began doubting myself and thinking back to my years as a teenager, and how I didn't focus on academics at all. I was confident in my job as a Green Beret. I could shoot, move, and communicate, but now, my family's livelihood would be based on my academics. I had so many negative thoughts that I struggled with severe anxiety.

In August 2011, I started the Reserve Officers' Training Corps (ROTC) at Campbell University in Fort Bragg, North Carolina. At the time, I was thankful that I had prepared for Ranger school because it refreshed my knowledge of small unit tactics. Much of the grading criteria for an ROTC cadet was how well you led, motivated, inspired, innovated, and communicated. Simply put, getting others to want to work together while achieving mission success.

I was fortunate to get paired with a great group of people, and several of us were in a unique situation. Campbell University is about forty minutes from Fort Bragg. The college had a satellite campus on-base which allowed us to attend many of our courses there. The ROTC program allowed cadets to conduct their ROTC courses at the school closest to them. For several of us, Methodist University was convenient. So we attended Campbell University for academics and Methodist University for ROTC. The Assistant Professor of Military Science (APMS) and an enlisted instructor at Methodist University were probably two of the top leaders in the entire ROTC program across the nation. My APMS had retired from the Army only a few years before I started. His experience and knowledge as an Army officer was extensive. For several of us, he became our mentor.

The active-duty program was a two-year course of instruction, and one of the requirements was the applicant must have previously completed two years of college. So, in my junior year, I did pretty well. Actually, we all did. Before starting the program, I had several conversations with my counselor about which degree program to choose. At the time, I wanted one where I was sure to be successful. The college had just introduced a degree in homeland security at several satellite campuses, but it had not been fully integrated at my location. Therefore, I chose history.

The ROTC courses, academics, physical fitness, and leadership were scored, and I received a grade for each, which provided an overall grade at the end of my junior year. We were also required to attend a month-long summer course; some call it summer camp. Everything in my junior year, along with the summer leadership course, was evaluated and provided me with an overall score. The scores were used in two ways; how I was ranked locally among my peers, and how I ranked nationally among more than four thousand cadets. Cadets competed for active duty slots, specific jobs, and permanent change of station (PCS) locations.

When I started the Green-to-Gold program, I was given a wish list of career fields and was required to rank them from highest to lowest based upon my preferences. My primary choice was the medical service corps. The medical field was vast, and locations were numerous, so I planned to take my special operations experience and merge it with a medical career and make lots of money once I left the U.S. Army. However, to be chosen as a medical corps officer, I had to be ranked in the top twenty percent of cadets nationally.

Once I made my choice, I also began to think about where I was going to be assigned. Up to that point in my career, Fort Bragg had been my only duty station; I had been there for thirteen years. My wife, Angel, and I discussed changing locations. We considered Europe or Hawaii, but at the time, we thought about our dogs being quarantined because of their breeds, which we did not want; so we decided not to pursue locations outside the U.S. The question we then asked ourselves was, "Which Army post do we want stateside?"

There were several factors also affecting my decision. As I aged, my body began to feel the aches and pains of being a hard charger. From the start of my military career, I had been jumping out of airplanes, carrying heavy weight on my back, running miles upon miles, climbing mountains in Afghanistan, and carrying heavy ammunition into AO's in Iraq. I believed if I stayed at Fort Bragg, I would be assigned to the 82nd Airborne Division. My thought was, *If I show up in the 82nd as a new second lieutenant and a former Green Beret, I will be challenged daily by every alpha male in the organization.* The questions would be; could I run faster than them, shoot better, climb a rope faster, etc. I did not want a job where every day, I had to relive the Special Forces selection process.

Finally, I returned from the summer leadership course and started my senior year. As a senior in the ROTC program, each cadet is given their assessment results and then a leadership position. During this year, we are required to lead and mentor junior cadets, just as we will do when we arrive at our first assignments as officers.

I was shocked when I received my test results; I had ranked number eighty in the entire USA. The ROTC permanent party cadre nominated me to be the cadet battalion commander. This started my senior year off very well, but it was October or November before I received my branch assignments. The day finally arrived, and I received my results; Medical Service Corps! Now that I was assigned a specific branch, I wasted no time contacting the branch manager. Also known as assignment officers, they manage personnel with the needs of the U.S. Army. Simply put, they tell you where you're going. However, if possible, they do work with you in fulfilling your preferences.

When I spoke with my branch manager, I shared my career history and how I was feeling physically. Thankfully, he had recently undergone back surgery due to injuries he received while he was an enlisted soldier. He sympathized with my situation and offered me a few suggestions, along with some options. He allowed me to choose five PCS locations. Angel and I discussed it and considered the two places which were outside the U.S. However, due to us having Rottweiler dogs, we ruled them out. We finally made a decision to move to our first option, Fort Hood, Texas. It all worked out fine. I was now going to be a medical service corps officer with an assignment at the 1st Medical Brigade located there. I was excited to finish my senior year. Everything had gone as planned, and there were no significant problems.

The month before graduation, we began finalizing our promotion ceremony. During the service as each cadet is promoted, it is a common tradition to render your first salute to an enlisted soldier or enlisted retiree and present them with a silver dollar. I remember thinking, *"Who do I want to ask?"* This was a big deal for me; I wanted to choose the right person. Then I thought, *"Angel's father, Robert!"* I remembered he was a former Navy enlisted man. He and I had a great relationship, and I really admired him. I called him at his home and asked if he'd do me the honor of receiving my first salute? Thankfully, he was excited and accepted my request.

Graduation and promotion came and went. That was indeed an

exciting time. Graduating from college was never something I saw for myself. I had wanted a college degree but never thought it was something I could achieve. I remember thinking, *"College degrees are for smart people."* I graduated Summa Cum Laude with a 3.9 GPA. Not bad for someone who had never crossed an academic stage before college.

Tragedy Before Moving

The time came for me to depart Fort Bragg and I was scheduled to attend the Basic Officer Leaders Course (BOLC) for the medical service corps, from July through September 2013. Angel decided she would visit her parents while I attended school. Her parents lived in Michigan, so visiting them would be more difficult once we moved to Texas because of the long distance. The day to depart came, and we hugged and kissed and said our goodbyes. Angel drove to Michigan, and I drove to Texas. The plan was for me to finish school, return to Fort Bragg, North Carolina; Angel would drive back from Michigan, and we would load the dogs and the remainder of our household goods and move to Fort Hood in Killeen, Texas.

I graduated from college in May 2013. Several weeks later, we received a call that Sylvia, Angel's mom, had fallen and was being placed in physical rehab. Sometime around August first, Angel called me and said that her father was very sick, and they were taking him to the hospital. Unfortunately, the doctors discovered Robert's cancer had returned, and his prognosis wasn't good. Thankfully, Angel had spent nearly twenty years in the medical field and was able to take care of her dad at home. We prayed fervently for his recovery, but there was no improvement. Finally, he was given only a few months to live. Angel's trip to Michigan went from a short term visit to long term in-home nursing care.

Angel spent much of her time transporting Robert to doctor appointments and visiting her mother, Sylvia, in the rehab center. It was a tough time for her, and whenever we talked on the phone, I tried to keep my conversations with her very positive. We kept praying for a miracle, and I truly believed that was going to occur. Finally, with Robert's health rapidly deteriorating, Angel called and said that I needed to fly up over the Labor Day weekend. Our fear was he might not live until my graduation date.

I flew up and spent a great weekend with the family. Thankfully, Robert was hanging in there, and then Angel said he wanted to talk to me. I recall sitting with Robert and talking about heaven and Jesus. I promised him that I would take care of his wife and his daughter. He was a man of few words, so he didn't say a lot, but I could tell he was grateful for my promise.

Once the weekend was over, I returned to Texas to finish my schooling. Angel and I kept praying for a miracle, and finally, God answered our prayers, but not the way we were expecting. The day before my last course finished, Angel called and said the rehab facility called her and said there was an urgent medical emergency with her mother. Not much was known about Sylvia's condition at the time, so we decided that it was best that I not book a flight to Michigan right away. Sadly, Sylvia passed away the next day. Everyone was aware of Robert's terminal condition, but Sylvia appeared to be okay. She was in the rehab facility for a relatively minor health condition.

After receiving the news about Sylvia, I told my instructors that my mother-in-law had died, then packed my bags and purchased a ticket to Michigan. Fortunately, my courses were nearly over. The instructors were very understanding and allowed me to leave early and still gave me credit for the classes. Arriving in Michigan, I was glad to see that Angel's family had everything under control. One of the saddest moments was taking Robert to his wife's funeral and watching him when he first saw Sylvia in the casket.

A few days after Sylvia died; Robert woke up in a lot of pain. Since he was already under hospice care, taking him to the hospital was not an option. Thankfully they had another place where he was sent and made comfortable. Robert's last days were filled with highs and lows. No one wanted to see him in pain any longer, but the thought of losing him along with Sylvia had created a gut-wrenching situation with Angel's family. Finally, the day everyone feared arrived. Angel and her immediate family were all together in the hospice room when Robert took his last breath and stepped into heaven.

Although both tragedies had just happened, I was still scheduled to report in early October to Fort Hood, Texas. I contacted my branch manager, informed him of the situation, and asked for an extension. It was granted, which gave us time to finalize the details in Michigan and get to Texas in time for me to report for duty.

Fort Hood, Texas Move
John's Story

"Welcome to the Great Place" were the first words my wife and I saw as we entered the main gate at Fort Hood. I thought, *"I hope this place truly is great."* For soldiers who have spent time in Fort Bragg, it's not uncommon to be frequently told the U.S. Army is different outside of Bragg. As a young soldier in the 82nd Airborne Division, we traveled to Army training centers and walked with our heads held high because we were from Fort Bragg. A lot of the bias and pride had left me while I was a Green Beret special operator, but it still crossed my mind entering the new base.

Because of Angel's recent family situation in Michigan, we hadn't contacted any realtors or home rental companies to find a house. It took a few days to find a place and get situated, but soon everything was okay. I was worried about Angel. In a short period of time, she had lost her brother, mother, and father, and now we were in a new place with no support system available to us. However, we did not feel completely alone because our North Carolina church pastor's daughter Nicki and her husband Kris had recently been stationed at Fort Hood. Once settled into our new home, I found Nicki's telephone number, knowing it would be good for us to be around familiar faces. After meeting with Kris and Nicki, they gave us pointers about the post and what they knew about the surrounding communities.

I started work around the first of November, 2013. I knew work was going to be a bit of an adjustment, but I was ready for the challenge. The last time I had managed young soldiers was before starting the Special Forces qualification course in 2003. As a Green Beret in an ODA, there are no soldiers below the rank of sergeant. Thankfully, ROTC provided a preview of what it was going to be like in a regular U.S. Army unit.

As I began processing into my company, I was excited to see the senior leaders were hard-chargers, i.e., leading by example. At my first meeting with Captain Cheatwood, my commanding officer, he asked me, "Why are you here?" What he really was saying was, "Why would someone leave the clandestine special operations community for the medical corps." I assured him I would work very hard and shared my motivation to become an Army officer and my plans for the future and, ultimately, retirement. I think there was a bit of relief on his part when I explained that to him. Alyse Trejo, our company executive officer (XO), became my mentor. Actually, both the commander and the XO were former enlisted as well. The first sergeant, who was the senior enlisted advisor to the commander, was a ball of fire and a former drill sergeant. Fitting in as a leader in the organization was seamless because of the excellent people around me.

My transition into the platoon was also just as great. The non-commissioned officers (NCOs) welcomed me because being former enlisted myself provided me with a bit of extra merit and legitimacy. All of the company cadre and members I met were very committed and a lot smarter than I was when I first joined the Army. Many of them also were very well educated. These soldiers were combat medics, which require an increased level of aptitude, ability, and skill.

As the new guy on the block, you are always being assessed by those in the unit, but your leading critics usually are the junior enlisted men and women. I remember, as a young soldier, we'd get a new lieutenant in our company, and no one would talk to them until after the first physical training (PT) session. Because they were un-officially being evaluated and we were challenging them, they had to earn our respect, and the clock started the first day at 6:30 am. In the Army, PT can set the tone for the day, your work assignment, and much more. I anticipated this situation in my new job and attempted to challenge them first. I didn't show up in the best of shape, but I did have enough physical conditioning to prove myself.

My new company had been short on staff for quite some time, which meant I had to learn fast, and there were several additional duties I needed to assume. One of those was the unit movement officer (UMO). This job required me to attend a few related courses and become certified. Unit movement officers plan and coordinate for their personnel and equipment to deploy by land, sea, or air. To be successful, those assigned this duty must be very meticulous and detail-oriented. I completed the UMO course and then started my second course, Transportation Coordinators' - Automated Information for Movements System II (TC-AIMS II). Now I was ready to begin what I believed was going be a long and successful career as a medical corps officer in the U.S. Army.

†††

CHAPTER SIX

Deadly Encounter
April 2, 2014

By early spring, Angel and I were settled into our new home and had our daily routines established. Angel started a new job with the local school district, and I was very happy for her because it helped take her mind off of her family. I knew the grieving process would take some time, and sitting at home with nothing to do was her worst enemy. Our weekend routine usually had us spending time with Nicki and Kris, or Captain Cheatwood and his wife, Kim. On Sundays, we went to Faith Point Church.

The week before, Pastor Dan and his wife Jan, from Rockfish Church, which we had attended in Fayetteville, NC, were in town visiting their daughter Nicki. I remember the excitement I felt upon seeing them. I admired Pastor Dan and thought it was a divine appointment that his daughter and her family were at Fort Hood with us. I believed we were there to start my career as an officer but also to be there for Kris and Nicki. The Sunday before Pastor Dan and Jan returned home, we all met for lunch. Away from everyone, I told Pastor Dan not to worry about Nicki and her family because Angel and I would help them in any way we could. Little did I know God's plan was actually the opposite; Kris and Nicki were stationed at Fort Hood to support Angel and me.

TC-AIMS training started, and I showed up at the late-morning class and sat on the front row. After a lengthy delay, the instructor started with the usual introductions and provided our class outline; however, by then, it was time for our lunch break. I spent my lunch talking to several school recruiters who were hosting a college fair at the building my course was in. After lunch, I returned to class, and the instructor told us he was going to let us leave early so that we could go to our units and copy our property books on to a compact disc. The course required that we complete a final project, and the instructor allowed participants to use their unit's actual information for the project. This gave the students a significant advantage when using TC-AIMS in the future.

When the class ended, I drove to my motor pool, thinking I would be able to get the transportation information I needed there. I spoke with a few warrant officers that sent me to my battalion supply section (S-4). En route, I called my sister Donna on my cell phone. We talked about the trip I had been planning for Angel and me to go to Cancun, Mexico. We had been there once before, and she loved it. She asked to go back as a way to get away after everything that had just happened with her brother and parents.

I drove through my battalion headquarters parking lot, but it was only four o'clock in the afternoon, and the mass departure for home after work had not yet started, which also meant there were no open parking spaces. I was forced to park near the brigade headquarters. I found a spot, pulled in, and told my sister I'd call her later. I was hurrying to get into the supply office before everyone left for the day. I stepped out of my vehicle and prepared to walk away. Then I suddenly heard what sounded like three or four rapid gunshots being fired. The shots quickly caught my attention and stopped me in my tracks.

Right in front of me where I had pulled up and parked, was a male soldier smoking a cigarette. After I heard shots being fired, I turned and looked at him and shrugged my shoulders, as if to say, "What was that?" I turned to look at the road that divided my unit and the motor pool of another one. I thought, *Maybe the shots were from soldiers firing blanks and practicing a twenty-one gun salute for ceremonies.* Then, a vehicle stopped in the parking lot, approximately fifteen feet in front of me. I glanced at the car and the soldier driving it but turned my attention back to the road where I had first heard the shots fired. At the time, I didn't believe I was in any danger because I was on one of the most secure military installations in America, and I wasn't in Afghanistan or Iraq.

The next shot I heard was followed by a .45 caliber bullet ripping through my throat, severing my left jugular vein, destroying my voice box, punching through my right brachial plexus (shoulder and arm nerve bundle), and breaking my scapula. The moment I was shot, I froze in unbelief. I wasn't sure what had just happened, I remember thinking, *"Am I shot?"* I didn't feel any neck pain, but it felt as if I had been hit in the chest with a baseball bat. Instantly, my worst fears were confirmed when I saw long thin streams of bright red blood spurting from my throat. My first reaction was to get away. I stumbled back to my car and then collapsed on the ground beside it. Thoughts began running through my mind, *"Is this it? Am I dying? What will happen to Angel and the kids? I don't think Angel can take any more loss."* Suddenly, I heard a strong voice tell me, *"Get up! Get up, or your wife will die!"* The voice didn't come from someone nearby. The voice came from within me and was very clear and powerful, with no urgency in its tone.

I tried to utter the name "Jesus." Pastor Dan Stanley from Rockfish Church in Fayetteville, NC, had told us, "When you pray, do so out loud." When I began to get up, it was as if God put Pastor Dan's words in my mind. I later realized that Jesus was telling me, "Call upon my name" because He knew I was about to face the enemy, once again and I would need a second miracle in the coming moments. I tried to pray, but all I could get out was "Jez." I couldn't even get Jesus's full name out. But, God knew what I had just done, and heaven in all its mighty glory was dispatched to help me.

I stood up and tried to cover my throat with my right hand, but realized my right arm wouldn't move and was just dangling by my side. I thought maybe it was broken when I first collapsed on the ground. As I explain the events now, it may seem that I was taking my time, but I can assure you my actions were happening in mere seconds, not minutes. Awkwardly using my left hand to grip my throat, I tried to stop the massive bleeding. There was no one around me, and I knew I needed help - fast. I began staggering toward my unit, hoping I could make it there before I passed out from loss of blood. Approaching the front door of the First Medical Brigade building, I saw a soldier in uniform walking toward me. I tried yelling for help. But nothing came out of my mouth but blood. As he and I drew closer to each other, something seemed strange about his movements. I thought, *"He's walking very calmly, but frantically looking around."* I stopped in my tracks, suddenly realizing, *"Oh my God. It is the shooter!"* He had fired at me from his car, and then drove away, parked, and was now walking directly toward me. There was nothing I could do; I couldn't run. We ended up approximately ten feet from each other, almost face-to-face. He stopped, quickly looked around, not even acknowledging that I was standing in front of him as if I was invisible. Then he turned, walked into the building, and killed one soldier and shot two others. Walking out the backdoor, he confronted an MP, and after they exchanged gunfire, Specialist Ivan Lopez killed himself.

I couldn't believe what had just happened, but I didn't stay around for him to walk back out as I stumbled toward my unit, and moved away from the brigade headquarters building. Then I heard someone yell to me, "Soldier, are you okay?" Later I was told that as I was walking, it appeared I had a red scarf flapping in the wind; because of the blood squirting from my neck. Stopping, I turned and weakly yelled back, "No, I've been shot. There's a shooter in headquarters." Disregarding their own safety, four soldiers ran over to me, yelling, "Get down." Those heroes were Staff Sgt. Borrego, Staff Sgt. Morales, Sgt. Amaro and First Lieutenant Hammond. They gently laid me between the parked vehicles as they carefully evaluated the situation. Staff Sgt. Morales later told me, You whispered in my ear, "He's in the brigade headquarters." The unit was alerted to the shooting by me announcing that I had been shot and sharing the shooter's location.

Thankfully several of the soldiers who rushed to my aid were medics. They realized the severity of my injuries and knew they had only moments to save my life, and there was no time to call 911 for an ambulance. There was no room for error; one wrong decision meant certain death for me. They quickly transported me to the hospital themselves. Sgt. Amaro ran to his pickup truck, which was located in the nearby parking lot, and drove it to where I was lying. They picked me up and laid me on the bed of the truck, and we heard the shooter still firing his weapon inside headquarters.

Darnell Army Hospital was only a short distance away, but it felt like we'd never get there. En route to the hospital, somebody was putting pressure on my throat to stop the bleeding. I attempted to move their hand away and say, "You're choking me," but no sound came not. It is a routine procedure when someone is bleeding to apply pressure to the wound to stop it. Unfortunately, I was bleeding from my throat, so when they applied pressure, it was hard for me to breathe. I shut my eyes during the ride so that I could focus on my breathing, and I would get an occasional slap in the face, followed by, "Stay with me, Sir." I could hear Staff Sgt. Borrego yelling at vehicles to get out of the way, and I'm sure many traffic laws were violated that day. Staff Sgt. Morales later said, "I was telling you not to speak but just squeeze my hand. As we drew closer to the hospital, your squeezing strength began rapidly to decrease."

Dried Blood—Mine

Beth Amaro, wife of Sgt. Amaro wrote about something she experienced the day after I was shot. She recalled, "The thick reddish-brown lines of Lieutenant Arroyo's dried blood had flowed in stripes down the white Texas license plate on our Dodge Ram pickup, and it paralyzed me when I first saw it. They ran down through the black letters and numbers and prevented me from seeing the license plate number. I stood there in silence for a moment, saddened by the reality of the previous day's events. I knew I had a short amount of time to remove as much dried blood as I could. I had to do it quickly because I did not want my husband, who had already spent several hours the night before washing the bed of the truck to wake up and see this. It would immediately bring back the event of the previous day in full force. Who was I kidding? Those images are, and would forever remain, embedded in his brain! I worked tirelessly with bleach and a scrub brush to clean and return the license plate to its normal state, quickly realizing there was blood pooled in the crevices of our bumper, but it was dark enough to hide it, and something a few more runs through the car wash would remove."

The Day John Is Shot
Angel's Story

John and I helped my sister and brother close up my parent's home and settle their affairs as much as we could, but soon it was time to say a final good-bye. As I left my family's house, I was sad because we found ourselves unattached to any other home. I drove back to North Carolina to retrieve our belongings at Fort Bragg then turned west to find a new home in Central Texas. We didn't have any friends or acquaintances there, so we were starting fresh. In God's usual, perfect way, He had brought a new spiritual commitment to John and a new birth for me at a time when we would be in a situation to find new friends, new associations, and new ways to build our lives.

We learned that our former pastor's daughter and her husband had just moved to the same area where we were going. They had already become a great strength in our new lives and a real place of connection. Arriving at Fort Hood, we found a place to live, I found a job I loved as a substitute teacher helping special needs children, and John settled into his new assignment. Everything was new. Death and pain were behind us. John had survived three tours of duty in war-torn Afghanistan and Iraq with no significant wounds. My emotional wounds began to heal because Jesus came into my life. Everything felt newer and more promising under the vast Texas sky. I began to feel safe as I settled into our daily routine. However, after six months of normal, routine life, suddenly a day came that changed everything, and we would never be the same.

It was Wednesday, April 2, 2014, and I never imagined I would experience a day like it. It was like any other of the many Wednesdays John and I shared. We had gotten up and gone to our jobs just like any other day. When I got off work at 3:00 pm, I came home and started preparing dinner for us so it would be ready around 6:00 pm when John usually got in. Around 4:00 pm, I received a phone call from Captain Cheatwood, John's commanding officer. "Hi, Angel. I was wondering, have you heard from John lately?" I was slightly puzzled by his question but figured there must have been a change in John's schedule or some other explanation. I answered, "No, I haven't. Usually, I don't hear from him until around 5:30 pm when he is on his way home. Do you want me to give him a message, then?" His response was for me to just have John call him. I didn't think any more about it and went back to the kitchen. Ten minutes later, my friend, Nicki, called and asked if I had heard the news about a mass shooting on the post. Since I don't watch the TV news, I told her I had no idea about what had happened. Then as soon as she told me there was a shooting in the post's medical area, it hit me. "That's why Captain Cheatwood was calling me." Everything in me panicked, and absolute terror began to consume me. Nicki tried to calm me down. Reassuring me that John probably was okay, she reminded me that he was always concerned for others, so he probably was busy helping out. I got off the phone with her in a complete state of shock. All I wanted was to hear from John! As I turned around and walked to the front room to turn on the TV, I looked through the glass storm door and saw Captain Cheatwood walking up to my front porch. *"No! No! No!"* Everything in me screamed. *"He can't be here. This is not possible. Nothing can happen to John. He isn't coming to notify me."* I froze in place, thinking, *"I will not open that door. If he can't come in, he can't tell me my husband is dead. I can just go finish supper, and John will be here in a minute; then, he can see that everything is okay."* I stood there unable to move, not breathing, blood rushing through my veins so intensely the sound of it roared in my ears. I saw Captain Cheatwood talking to me, but I refused to hear what he was saying. Finally, forcing air into my lungs, I took a breath, and listened to his words, "He's alive! Angel, John's alive! Please let me come in, we need to get you to the hospital immediately so that you can be with him." My knees weakened, my eyes overflowed with tears, but every fiber of my being rose up and shouted, *"Thank You, God!"*

An air ambulance flew John from Darnall Hospital on Fort Hood to Baylor, Scott and White Hospital in Temple, Texas, where trauma equipment capable of saving his life was located. Arriving in Temple, Captain Cheatwood, his wife, and I had to wait until John was stable enough for us to go in to see him. I used all of that time to pray and to visit with a priest who had come to talk to me. Finally, it was time for me to go in and see him. But before I could go back to the intensive care room, I was told by the hospital staff, I had to describe my husband. The only thing I could think of to say was, "He's a short Mexican guy with lots of tattoos." Then they asked me to describe the tattoos. So I told them about the one he had across his stomach that he got long-ago as a gang member. I wanted to say to them that the tattoos no longer defined him, but I didn't have time to explain. But it was enough verification to get me back to see him, and that was all I wanted.

I held it all together pretty well until I walked into John's intensive care unit (ICU) room. When I saw John, I totally lost it. It was overwhelming to see him on the bed with all kinds of tubes coming from him. His head was swollen as big as a basketball, which caused his tongue to stick out. I was devastated to see my husband so critically impacted by such a senseless act of violence. Why would anyone shoot him? How could this have happened on a secure military post in the United States? I had a feeling that I would never be safe again. No matter where I was.

I was allowed only a short visit with him, and then, they sent me home. But after only a couple hours of sleep, my need to be with my husband was much stronger than my physical need for rest. So, Nicki took me back to the hospital. John was in surgery when we arrived, and sitting in the waiting room while they finished was agonizing for me. After the surgery, his doctor told me they were putting him in a medically induced coma to give his body the complete rest it needed so he could heal. Even though he was in a coma, back at his hospital room, I sat down next to him, grasped his hand, and started telling him how much I loved him. He instantly responded by widely opening his eyes, looking directly at me, and trying to sit up and talk. The doctors quickly came into the room and got him back "under," but that brief moment helped my heart so much. I needed to see my husband respond to the love I was feeling for him. It helped to sustain me for the long days ahead during his recovery.

The flood of family and friends that came to the hospital over the next few days was a fantastic show of concern and support for John and for me. Baylor Scott and White in Temple was a great hospital. Not only did the staff put John's health and recovery first and foremost, but they also made allowances for the large numbers of visitors who arrived to see us every day. They increased the number of people who could go into his room from two to four, letting him have visitors most of the day, and they gave us another nearby room so we could gather and visit there in between seeing John. They clearly understood the healing that happens for patients when they know they are loved and cared about.

Six days later, the medical staff decided that John was stable enough to be moved to San Antonio for continued treatment. I saw this as a good, hope-giving sign, so I began to make plans to go there as well. Then I was told that President Obama was coming to Fort Hood in two days, and he wanted to meet with all the family members of the ones who had been impacted by the shooting. While I appreciated the gesture the President was making, I didn't want to meet with him if it meant letting my husband go to San Antonio without me. John's transfer was delayed until after the President's visit. When I met with the President's secretary, she said, "Oh, so you are the Arroyo family. I was on the phone all night, making sure that they did not move your husband until after this visit."

A life-flight helicopter flew John to San Antonio's Brooke Army Medical Center. I made the trip by car in a little over two and a half hours and was glad that I didn't get lost in the heavy traffic as I tried to find it. However, once inside the immense hospital, I got so lost I was afraid that I would never find my way to John. With help from the hospital staff, I found his room and stayed with him for several days. Once I was assured that he was healing and being well taken care of, I decided to return to my home and job in Killeen and the responsibility of caring for our four dogs and two birds. John now was in good hands, so I made the two and a half-hour drive every weekend, this allowed me to keep my job and still spend time with him. After approximately a month, he was doing much better and was released to go to the nearby Fisher House. This was a facility that housed eight families who each had their own rooms and shared a common area and kitchen while their family member was still recovering. John was scheduled to go there at the end of April. The only problem was that he had to have a caregiver to help him dress and to change his bandages and keep his wounds clean. I couldn't keep my job and be there every day with John. It was vitally important for me to keep my job until we knew the outcome of John's recovery. As I considered those who were close to us that could possibly help, I realized that everyone had obligations that prevented them from coming to San Antonio. Everyone that is, except for one person. Our son Mason came to mind. He was in a low paying job in Michigan, and I wanted to get him out of that job and environment. When I shared what I considered to be a great idea and solution with John, he began vehemently to shake his head from side to side. "No! No!" his motions emphatically said.

It is an understatement to say that John and Mason were not the best of friends. But time was short, and we really didn't have any other options. I called Mason that evening, and he was on the highway the next day, headed to help John. He dropped off his girlfriend and her daughter with me, so I got to know Allison and Madison better. Mason stayed with John during the week, and then we traded places on the weekends when I stayed with John and Mason stayed at our home with Allison and Madison. During this time, the relationship between Mason and John was healed, and they became best friends. It is incredible to watch what happens when God moves in hearts and brings healing to relationships.

Darnall Army Hospital
John's Story

I remember arriving in the emergency area of the hospital and being put on a gurney. I recall a lot of commotion and a sense of urgency then someone put an oxygen mask on my face. Once it was in place, I remember feeling safe, and my body began to relax, and then I passed out. That's the last I remember at Darnall Hospital on Fort Hood. Much of what happened next has been shared with me by those who transported me, and nurses and doctors with whom I later spoke. What was told to me is that one of the doctors in the ER made a critical decision. Upon examining me, he immediately inserted a curved plastic tube down my throat, so I had a clear passageway to breathe. My neck was beginning to swell rapidly, and my airway was quickly closing, so the decision to intubate me saved my life. Many of the staff were surprised that the doctor was even able to get a tube down my throat with the massive amount of damage I had sustained.

The ear, nose, and throat (ENT) surgeons had just completed a routine surgery for the day when they received an intercom page informing them of my arrival, which caused them to sprint to the emergency room. Dr. Alex McKinley later told me, "When Dr. Reed and I exited the elevator and were running towards the ER, the nurses were running toward the elevator, pushing you on a gurney. In the elevator, I could see your neck quickly swelling. We knew it was a critical time. You were losing an enormous amount of blood, so we started working on stopping the bleeding. I remember thinking, *"We can lose this guy at any second."*

I frequently reflect back on the miraculous sequence of events that day. I was shot point-blank, heard the voice of Jesus tell me to get up, stand only ten feet from the shooter before realizing it is him. Then medics came to my aid and rushed me to the hospital, where a doctor intubates me, as the nurses are running to the elevator with me and the ENT surgeons are running from the elevator towards my gurney. Everything which was necessary for my survival from the instant I was shot was precisely where it needed to be.

As all this was happening with me, Angel was at home preparing dinner, unaware that she may lose her husband at any second. Simultaneously, the media heard about the second Fort Hood mass shooting, and the event became breaking news worldwide.

Angel said when she arrived at the hospital and first saw me, I was unrecognizable. She wasn't sure if the man lying on the hospital bed was her husband. She later told me that my head was bigger than a basketball, and my tongue was swollen so large that it would not fit inside my mouth. At the time, many people were praying for me, but clinically speaking, I was living minute-to-minute. Lieutenant Hammond later told me, "After we got you to the hospital, I called my wife to let her know I was okay and shared that we got one of the victims to the hospital, but he was probably dead by now." Many nurses, doctors, and those who happened to be in the area said that I should have died that day!

Once Angel composed herself, she knew she had to contact my family. She called my mother and told her what had happened. When Angel made the phone call, the doctors were not entirely sure of the extent of my injuries. I was told my mom fainted when she heard the news. Mom contacted my sister Donna and provided what little information she had. Donna contacted the remainder of my family to include my son John, Jr. My brother's wife, Monic, took charge of communicating with my friends via Facebook. My family quickly began to book their flights, and by Thursday afternoon, they were arriving in Texas.

Baylor Scott & White Hospital Transfer

Thursday, April 3rd, I was still alive, and the doctors were hopeful I would survive, but I wasn't yet entirely out of danger. By now, the news had been circulating across most social media platforms. Prayer requests were going out around the world. Angel's phone was ringing non-stop, with everyone wanting to know what happened and what could they do to help us. Our friend Nicki quickly rushed to Angel's side, taking over her phone and dealing with everything that Angel could not handle at that time. Nicki also reached out to Faith Point Church's senior pastors, Scott and Marsha Hoxworth. Faith Point was the church we had been attending in Killeen, Texas. That wonderful church was just getting to know us, but that didn't matter to them; they treated Angel and my family as if we had been members for many years. The pastors rushed to my side while the church started a corporate prayer for us, as well as providing meals for Angel and those who were staying at my house. The support we received from Faith Point church was fantastic.

Captain Cheatwood went back and forth daily from my hospital room to the company area. Not only did he have a soldier fighting for his life, but he was still a company commander, and many of our soldiers were emotionally affected by the attack. He had to address their needs as well. Thankfully, we had an outstanding executive officer, First Lieutenant Trejo, who coordinated everything for my family. By the time they landed, she had arranged to have a vehicle and a driver for them, and rarely left my family's side. I can only speculate, but I'm sure she did not get much sleep that week. If she wasn't with my family, she was coordinating housing and meals on their behalf. Then she'd take them to the hotel and come to the hospital and sit with me.

By Thursday afternoon, I was going in for my second surgery at Baylor Scott & White hospital. Angel, Nicki, and a few others had been staying in my ICU room. I returned from my second surgery, and the doctors told Angel that I was going to be placed in a medically induced coma until Saturday. I have heard that people in a coma can hear but not talk. I can tell you first hand that I could hear people speaking all around me, but I could not respond. I wasn't sure if I was dreaming or not. Angel walked to my bed, grabbed my hand, and said that she loved me, and I woke up. It was a miracle!

I remember opening my eyes and trying to figure out what had happened. I attempted talking and moving my right arm, but I couldn't. I opened my eyes just in time to see my mother, sister Donna and Monique, brother Steve, and cousin Marlene walk in my room. It seemed like every time I closed my eyes, I would wake up to someone new arriving in my room.

Fort Hood's senior leaders visited me, including General Mark Milley, who was the commander of III Corps and Fort Hood. Today he is the military's top General, holding the position of Chairman of the Joint Chiefs of Staff. Texas Governor Rick Perry and Senator Ted Cruz stopped in to see me as well. Honestly, there were more visitors than I can remember.

When General Milley stopped in, I noticed he was wearing a Special Forces tab. For the uninformed, it is a service school qualification tab worn on military uniforms. While General Milley was talking with me, I pointed at his Special Forces tab and was trying to tell him I had one of those, and that I was a Green Beret as well. He looked at his tab and said, "Do you want that?" I moved my mouth with no words coming out, but I was saying, "I have my own." He generously took the tab off and gave it to me!

I couldn't believe it, but many of my closest friends flew or drove in from across the nation. Ivan and Carlos flew in from the West Coast. James arrived from Colorado. Chad and Crystal drove in from El Paso. Sonny, Adam, Makeeka, Darren, Steve, and Julie came from North Carolina. Victor and his family drove up from San Antonio. I was overwhelmed by the love everyone expressed. The hospital staff at Baylor Scott and White went above and beyond the routine care to help my family and the families of the other victims. They provided a separate waiting room for my family and stocked it with food.

Questions

Several days after the shooting, I had a lot of questions. The questions that perplexed me the most were: Whose voice did I hear telling me to get up? Was it mine, or was it the audible voice of Jesus? Why didn't I die that day? No one gets shot in the throat with a .45 caliber bullet from fifteen feet away and lives to tell about it. Why did the voice tell me to get up or my wife will die? Would I ever speak again, and what's the extent of the injuries to my right arm? Who were the soldiers that saved me, and will they be recognized for their heroic act?

The lead ear nose and throat surgeon at Baylor Scott and White told me that he expected I would fully recover. I was excited to hear that, but for others that saw my condition, it was hard to believe. I couldn't speak, and the initial reports were: I might have lost my voice forever. I remember telling my commander the doctors said I would make a full recovery, and I was expecting to be back to work in about three months. I told Pastor Scott the same news. He gave me a questioning look that conveyed, "Are you sure?" I don't know how I did it, but I was able to mumble, "Full recovery pastor." I think he was surprised when I said that, but he knew that God was working in my life.

I received my cell phone back once the military police investigation was over and cleared the crime scene. Once I turned my phone on, it beeped and constantly buzzed, letting me know that I had numerous saved messages. They were from everyone who had been trying to contact me during the shooting and those who had been watching the breaking news calling to make sure I wasn't a victim. Tina, a close friend of Angel's and mine, sent me a text message about an encounter she had with Jesus as she was praying for me the evening I was shot. She told me she was crying out to God, begging him to spare my life. Her prayer was a mixture of frantic pleading and overwhelming tears. As Tina was praying, she heard a voice say to her, "John is going to be okay." Tina said, "I never had experienced anything like this before, so I shrugged it off." She went back to her prayer, and again the voice said, "John will be okay, he has much work to do for me. John tells everyone about Jesus, and because of that, I'm going to use him." Tina said, "The second time I heard the voice, it left me speechless but with an overwhelming feeling of peace." She said she could not explain it, but she instantly knew I would fully recover and be okay.

I talked to my commanding officer Captain Cheatwood. He said, "Through this entire situation, my faith in Christ has been restored." I asked him what he meant. He said, "I know that I witnessed a true miracle. I'm a former Army medic. I know what that bullet did to you, and you shouldn't be here today." Other stories like Captain Cheatwood's and Tina's began to be told to Angel and me. Not only stories, but miracles were also happening. Thursday, when I opened my eyes, I tried to sit up and eventually did! My sister Donna told me, "The nurses had tears in their eyes because they couldn't believe what they were seeing." People who came to visit me walked into my room expecting to see someone on the verge of death, but surprisingly I was sitting up attempting to communicate with them, and death had been overcome. Donna also describes the shock and amazement on the faces of the Fort Hood surgeons who worked on me, Doctors McKinley and Reed. When they walked into my room, they weren't expecting to see me sitting up, trying to communicate with them. She said one of the doctors was holding his cell phone in his hand, almost trembling because she thought he wanted to ask if he could take a picture of me, but never did ask.

God began to speak to me, saying, *"John, that was my voice. You didn't have the power to get up. When you heard my voice it was accompanied with every bit of strength you needed to get up, but I'm not the one that picked you up, you had to make the decision whether to live or not. You have been asking, "Why did I hear get up, or my wife will die? If you did not get up that one bullet would have killed you and Angel. Angel would not have been able to endure any more loss. Do you remember standing ten feet from the shooter, face-to-face, after he shot you? I blinded him so that he wouldn't see you."*

As God revealed His answers to me, it wasn't like He walked into my room as a visitor, and then I began to take notes. These were spiritually responses he was giving me. It was like being a school-child and learning math, 2+2 = 4. As God began to reveal these answers to me, and later many more, I knew it was the truth.

The commander of the U.S. Army Southern Region Medical Command came to visit me. Major General Jimmie O. Keenan, a wonderful woman, was in charge of every medical facility in the southern region of the United States, and Fort Hood was in the heart of the south. My family having no experience with the military did not understand the rank structure at all. So when people came into my room, they didn't know the difference between a sergeant, a colonel, or a general. My mother described Major General Keenan as the woman soldier who came into my room and was crying. My family didn't know that who they were hugging and crying with was one of the senior generals in Army medicine. MG Kennan not only walked into my room as a leader, but as a fellow soldier, a mother, and a daughter. My family never saw her rank or even knew what a major general was during their encounter. What they saw was her heart!

MG Keenan spoke with me and asked if I would like to be transferred to San Antonio, TX. It is the location of the San Antonio Medical Military Center (SAMMC), which is the military's Level I Trauma Center in the southern region. Struggling to speak words, I hoarsely squeaked out, "Yes!" When I was a student the summer before attending the officer basic course, I heard about the many miracles that had occurred at SAMMC and the Center for the Intrepid rehabilitation facility, which is located on its campus. Knowing that she had driven up from San Antonio, I told her that I was willing to go back with her in the government van. Everyone was thankful for what Baylor Scott and White Hospital had done, but the military had adequate facilities to take over now.

MG Keenan set the process in motion to have me transported to SAMMC. I was scheduled to be moved on April 9, 2014. Then we learned that President Obama was coming to Fort Hood on the same day to host a memorial service for the personnel who were killed. The White House staff was asking that all families of the victims be present at the ceremony. My family acknowledged the invitation but sent a regret that they would not be attending because I was being transported to San Antonio that same day. However, behind the scenes, things were happening because transporting me to SAMMC was delayed by one day so my family could attend the ceremony. Lieutenant Trejo escorted them to the service.

The President and his wife, Michelle, individually met with each family. The Army's senior leaders also arrived from Washington and met with the families as well. My son John, Jr. talked with President Obama and mentioned that he was in school studying business. The truth is he was actually preparing to start school. I often joke with him that the Secret Service was looking for him because he had lied to the President of the United States. My sister Donna tells the story of being embarrassed about what she was wearing when she met the President and First Lady. My family wasn't expecting to attend any formal services, so in their haste to get to Texas, they just threw a few items in a suitcase and quickly boarded an airplane. Donna jokingly talks about the day she met the President of the United States, she was wearing her tennis shoes!

SAMMC Recovery

On April 10, 2014, I was transported in a life-flight helicopter from Baylor Scott & White Hospital in Temple, Texas, to San Antonio Medical Military Center (SAMMC), and my family returned to their homes. Angel stayed at Fort Hood to get things in order and look after our house. I'm not really sure where I was located within SAMMC hospital for the first few days. What I do remember is there was a nurse seated next to me the entire time. Then, I was told that access to my room and to me personally, was restricted due to the nature of the incident.

The first time I realized my military career was probably ending was when the commander of the Warrior Transition Battalion (WTB) stopped in to see me. Lieutenant Colonel Eric Edwards told me that at some point, I probably was going to be transferred to his command. At the time, I had very little knowledge of the WTB. However, I thought that was where the Army sent soldiers before they left the military. I wasn't ready to get out of the U.S. Army because I had just become a commissioned Army officer, and my career wasn't finished. Therefore, I wasn't too excited about talking to someone from the WTB.

A few days passed by, and I was moved to a permanent hospital room. Actually, I was moved into the penthouse of the hospital, designated "Suite 7T." Once there, I was included in the early morning medical residents' stampede. What that means is: new doctors going through their residency training from the different clinics all came into my room before sunrise, checked on me, and discussed any upcoming procedures for that day or anything else that was pertinent to my immediate recovery. At least that's what's supposed to happen. What really occurs is that I was awakened starting at "zero dark thirty," and they all began talking to me while I was still groggy and could not understand much of what was said; then they rushed out of the room and were gone. That happened every day!

General Milley stopped in to see me one morning, and I was not having a particularly good day. I did not think that I was getting any real answers on the condition of my nearly paralyzed right arm. The resident stampede had come and gone, and I was frustrated. The head nurse from my floor told me I should make a list of my concerns, and they would page the clinics to send representatives to my room to discuss each of them with me. I made my list and was waiting for the clinic representatives to come when General Milley stopped by. He walked in, and of course, the senior hospital leadership was accompanying him. He asked me how I was doing, along with making some small talk. It was hard for me to communicate because I couldn't talk, but my nurses were always there to help because we had learned to converse together. I grabbed my list, looked at my nurse, and tried to tell her to share this with the general. He grabbed my list and began reading each one of my written concerns and then stopped to hear how the hospital staff planned to respond to them. Before leaving, he gave me his email address and told me if I had any issues with my care to contact him. Needless to say, it wasn't long after he left that I had numerous visitors come to my room, fully answering all of my questions.

When the bullet tore through my throat, it also went through my right shoulder, stopping in my back without exiting. After a few days of staying at SAMMC, I began to get a painful, pinching sensation where the bullet was lodged. I told my doctors that when I laid down flat on my back, it was very uncomfortable. They took x-rays and confirmed that, in fact, it was the bullet embedded there and scheduled me for surgery. It was extracted, which was a relief. However, what surprised me is that I never got to see the bullet or keep it as a souvenir. I was told it had to be sent back to Fort Hood for evidence. What evidence? The shooter had killed himself!

While I was in the hospital, I was astounded by how easily people found me. I guess it wasn't too hard since my incident made headlines around the world. One of my best days was when Master Sergeant Trent, a Green Beret from the Special Operations Care Coalition, walked into my room and said, "We received a phone call from Fort Bragg and Special Operations Command (SOCOM) in Florida, telling us that you are a Green Beret. We are here to help!" I cannot adequately explain the range of emotions I had when he came into my room, and I learned that my brothers in the special operations community still had my back even if I wasn't a part of their formation. It was a very humbling experience for me.

Life changed drastically for Angel and me. We tried to figure out how to manage it all. Just because I was injured didn't mean I could focus only on myself or my injuries. Actually, for me, the burden got worse because I felt helpless in meeting the needs of my family. Generally, I was the one that worked through the more difficult situations that were before us. But in this situation, Angel was forced to step into that role. She was driving back and forth from Killeen to San Antonio, which is approximately two hours each way. On the nights she stayed with me in the hospital, she snuggled up to me in my bed, unless we had a strict nurse that would ask her to sleep in the foldout bedside chair. We were in a very unsettled situation at this time. It looked like my career was soon going to end. Angel and I were living in two different locations, and we didn't know how long we were going to be separated.

My time in the hospital was coming to an end, and everything I needed in those few weeks had been done. It was time for long-term recovery. As we began preparing for me to leave the hospital, we learned that I needed a non-medical attendant (NMA) to help me, or I wouldn't be released. NMA's are trained by the nursing staff to care for wounds and injuries that don't necessarily require hospitalization. The main question Angel and I had was, "Who would this person be?

Angel was learning to communicate with me because I had no voice at the time, and we didn't know when, or if, it would come back. Who would be able to understand or talk with me if it wasn't Angel? We had many questions and not a lot of answers. Another big concern for us was if Angel moved down to San Antonio to be near me, who would watch our dogs, and take care of our house?

Without letting our current situation overwhelm us, we embraced our faith as much as we could. Angel and I frequently prayed together. Then I would pray by myself, and she would pray by herself. We also had others around the world praying for us too. I thought, *"If God picked me up off the ground, then He was going to see me through this."*

Angel came to me one day and said, "God told me to have our son Mason be your NMA." Although I couldn't speak, my immediate response to her statement was an emphatic, "No! Absolutely not Mason!"

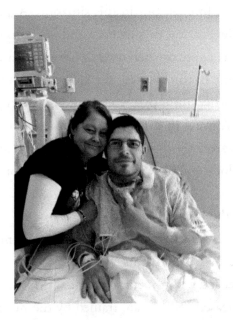

John & Angel at Baylor Scott & White

General Milley Gives John a Nuggie

John With General Dempsey & Wife

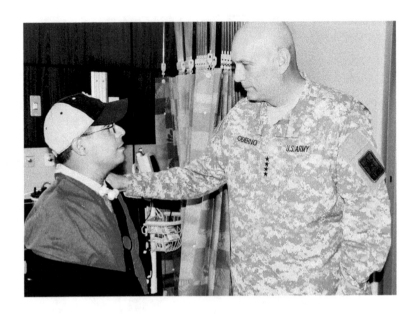

John with General Odierno

John's Family With Obama's

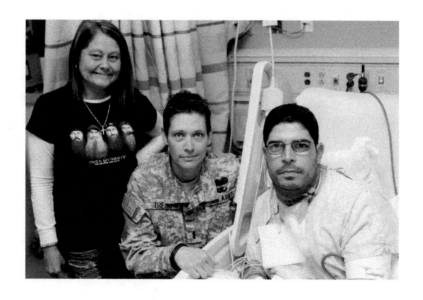

Angel & John with 1LT Trejo

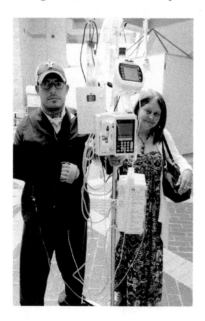

Walking the Hallways at BAMC

†††

CHAPTER SEVEN

Mason, My NMA

Mason and I previously had a troubled relationship. First of all, when he was growing up, I was not a good role model. When he was a teenager, I was there for him some, but I could have spent a lot more one-on-one time with him. Then in 2006, Mason was thirteen years old and had begun to get in trouble. We caught him smoking cigarettes and hanging out with the wrong crowd. During that time, Angel was a nurse working twelve-hour shifts from 7:00 am to 7:00 pm. I had moved from my Special Forces detachment because of a motorcycle injury and was forced to take a desk job at my battalion headquarters. Then I took on a second job, which started immediately after I left my job at the battalion. Sometimes I wouldn't get home until 9:30 pm or 10:00 pm. Our teenage children were home by themselves for a few hours after school before Angel got there. During that time, Mason was getting into more trouble. Back then, I blamed Mason's friends for his problem behavior, which really strained our relationship. God gave me an ultimatum during that time. He said, *"You can have your family, or you can have more money, but you cannot have both."* Regrettably, I chose the money, and my family suffered and began to unravel. Then in April 2014, I found out that I needed a fulltime NMA, and God tells Angel that Mason will be the one for the job.

With all our support system, there wasn't anyone willing to put his or her life on hold to babysit me. There were a lot of unknowns: i.e., how long did I need an NMA? Did I have to live in the Warrior Transition barracks? Could I stay at the Fisher House? Did I have to go back to Fort Hood for my recovery? Would the Army transition me to Fort Sam Houston? How long will Angel have to drive back and forth?

A day later, Angel came back to me and said Mason was willing to be my NMA for as long as it takes. She also said that we didn't have any other options. What was I going to say? We needed all the help we could get. Besides, Angel was taking care of everything at this point, and it would have added additional stress on her if I put up a fight, so I grudgingly relented.

We told the hospital that Mason was going to be my NMA. I was assigned an inpatient nurse case manager to assist us. She wasted no time getting Mason's official orders cut and really got things moving. Master Sergeant Trent from the SOCOM care coalition arranged for us to move into a Fisher House room. We waited for Mason to arrive from Michigan because I could not be discharged from the hospital until my NMA was present. Waiting for Mason also meant that I had a few extra nights staying in the hospital penthouse. Several of the top Army commanders were scheduled to visit me, and the hospital staff did not want to have to search for me outside the large hospital.

One day a visitor and I were catching up on some small talk, and I told him General Ordierno was supposed to stop by sometime that day. I said, "Don't be surprised if he walks in while you're here." Within a few minutes, four-star General Ordierno walked in the room, followed by his aides and senior hospital officials. General Ordierno is six feet six inches tall, which is somewhat intimidating. There was no advance notice that he was en route. Suddenly, he walks into my room. My visitor and I turn and see someone enter, and there in front of us is this tall man with four stars on his uniform standing there. My visitor instinctively snapped to attention, and I'm not sure how it came out, but he calls the empty room to attention, but it sounded very low pitch, like when someone gets startled. That was one of the funniest moments I had while in the hospital. After being shot, I decided not to be so serious all the time, even when it's the Army's top commanders in front of you.

The last VIP who visited me was the military's ranking general, General Martin Dempsey, Chairman of the Joint Chiefs of Staff. He stopped in with his lovely wife. I had grown accustomed to being around military and civilian leaders of high rank, and usually, had a casual attitude around them and was not so uptight. When I met General Dempsey, I thought, *"He's our senior leader, I better stand at attention."* Getting out of bed, I was standing at attention in my baggy pajamas, which was a little goofy, and he knew I was just trying to make light of the situation. He and his wife just laughed with me. I'm sure that was a bit of a pucker factor for some of the other hospital leaders with him, but no one said anything to me. For the most part, everyone was sincerely concerned about my well-being and the welfare of my family

Hospital Discharge

Mason arrived in Texas the week of April 21, 2014. By Thursday the 24th, the nurses had trained him on how to care for my wounds. My inpatient case manager believed it was best if I had a home nurse check on me a few times each week since Mason was new to wound care management. So she had everything coordinated before I was discharged. On April 25th, Mason and I moved our things into one of the Fisher House residences. I still was unable to speak, so communicating with people was tough. It helped that I had a white dry erase board which I carried with me, and it didn't take long for Mason and me to create our own way of communicating.

April 25th was on a Friday, so after moving into the Fisher House, I decided to return to Fort Hood for a weekend visit. I wasn't sure how I was going to react emotionally, but I knew I had to go home sometime. I felt a strong urge to visit the place where I was shot. As Angel and I were driving on post getting closer to that awful location, I remember my heart began to race. Getting out of the truck, my palms began to sweat, my heart was pounding, and yet it wasn't as severe as I thought it would be.

What happened on that deadly afternoon quickly returned to my mind. I remembered everything, and it was like each aspect was replaying in my head. I walked out the complete scenario from hearing the shots being fired, to the shooter driving up, me being shot, collapsing next to my car, then getting up, standing face-to-face with the shooter, and finally, my rescuers racing me off to the hospital. The cleanup crew must have done a great job because I saw no blood on the ground, and I know that I lost three-quarters of my blood volume on that ground. Before we left the parking lot, I went back and stood on the very spot I was shot, and I began to pray, claiming victory over what Satan tried to do to me. Jesus had revealed to me why I was to go back there only a short time after I had been shot. He said, *"For you to move forward, you must go back to the place you nearly died and take all authority away from the enemy."* Because Jesus walked alongside me, my level of anxiety I thought I was going to have, turned out not to be very severe.

After the weekend, I returned to San Antonio and began in-processing at the Warrior Transition Battalion (WTB). Mason was by my side every step of the way. He was mostly my voice at a time when I was physically unable to speak. He provided me with fantastic support and quickly caught on to what the nurses taught him and was patient and gentle with me. Our Fisher House room was no larger than your standard hotel room with twin beds. It was just the two of us, together with each other day after day, and night after night. The Lord knew exactly what he was doing by putting Mason and me together during that time.

Frankly, God humbled me before Mason. I was broken before my son, continually telling him, "Thank you for helping me." Mason controlled everything in this situation, but instead of bringing up the past, he extended grace and mercy to me. Over the next two and one-half months, when Mason and I lived in that small room, Jesus restored our relationship. He not only began by physically healing me, He also began healing all my other relationships as well. John Arroyo, the hardened Green Beret, before April 2nd, did not get up off the ground; but Jesus's ambassador and disciple did, and there was more work needing to be done, including restoring the relationship with our son Mason.

I left the hospital with the tracheostomy in my neck, which was in place to help me breathe, and a feeding tube attached to my stomach. My ear nose and throat doctor wasn't sure if my voice would ever return. Additionally, his initial timeframe for the trach being removed was estimated to be in about six months. There was still a lot of swelling around my throat, and I was unable to breathe without the trach.

A few days after my hospital discharge, my ENT doctor decided that it was okay for me to start trying to talk. He changed some type of hardware in my trach, which allowed me to push out sounds. I was instructed to speak as little as possible because there was a lot of healing still happening in my neck. At first, I quickly could tell if I overdid it because I began to feel as if my throat was closing up, and I would lose my voice. It didn't take much for that to happen.

The first day I was allowed to speak, I called my family. When my sister Donna answered her phone, she was shocked, realizing that it was me on the other end. Although my voice was scratchy, cracking, and hoarse, it was still me! She told me later, "I was confused. Why is my brother's phone calling me?" When she heard my voice, she began to cry, realizing that she was listening to a miracle. Some of the first reports my family received after I was shot was my voice box had been blown out. Everyone around me watched as Jesus continued working daily miracles in my body.

My day-to-day routine in the WTB started with an accountability meeting in the morning, then various appointments for the remainder of the day. I was assigned a nurse case manager to help with booking my appointments and making sure I met my medical goals and career objectives. Psychologists, therapists, and counselors who specialized in assisting mass shooting survivors were first on the list of mental health care providers with whom I met. There were a lot of questions that needed to be answered. I had been in combat three times and made it home without major life-threatening injuries. But on a random day, on one of the most secure installations in the world, nineteen soldiers were shot by someone wearing our uniform. One of the first things I realized was that there weren't many places that made me feel safe anymore.

The counseling helped me overcome many of my fears, and it also helped my wife Angel with the grief from losing both parents, and her anxieties about my current situation. I knew that I would eventually have to deal with my feelings towards the soldier who shot me. That question finally came from the Center for the Intrepid behavioral health Specialist Jorge, when he asked me, "How do you feel towards the shooter?" I remember taking a deep breath and letting my feelings out as I said, "I have no animosity towards him, nor do I hate him, as a matter of fact, I pray for his family, and I hope that one day I can tell them that my family and I have no bitterness towards them whatsoever." I also remember thinking, *"I believe his wife and children were victims as well. I cannot explain why I have those feelings towards him. Most people would have some hostility towards the person that shot them, but for me, it is quite the opposite. When Jesus told me to get up off the ground, I believe He took away all my bitterness, hate, and anger because He knew for me to work on his behalf, my heart had to be filled only with love."*

The way I feel now is, "How can I be upset or sad? I have been given another day on earth with my wife, children, family, and friends. I'm not angry, but thankful for what I have. Hate and animosity will only destroy me." Not everybody will understand what I have just said, but if you have experienced a comparable circumstance and are on a similar assignment from Jesus, you will appreciate my new found attitude.

After being shot, I was a different person, and it has taken some time for me to overcome my fear of being randomly and unexpectedly attacked. Let me explain my struggle. Early in my recovery as I walked by people, I sometimes wondered if the person that just passed would attempt to shoot me in the back. Also, if a vehicle drove slowly by me, I would wince when I saw it. Those reactions were happening mostly on the Army post. Even today, I avoid crowded areas, especially if I feel an active shooter will have an advantage. Sadly, active shooters are not our only threat. The term really should be "active aggressor" because not everyone is using guns these days. I still battle a few residual emotions and concerns from the incident, but my faith in Jesus will see me through my struggles. Thankfully I have had wonderful support.

One of my first questions about my future was, "Do I want to continue on active duty?" Depending on my decision, my recovery plan needed to meet my immediate medical needs while I was processing through a medical evaluation board (MEB) and transitioning into medical retirement and future healthcare needs met through the Veterans Administration. Secondly, should I remain on active duty status while working towards returning to a medical corps assignment someday?

Honestly, remaining on active duty was never a question for me. God knew what He created when I was born, and quitting was not a part of my DNA. My goal was to finish what I started and to ensure I did my best to achieve financial security for my family. *(Note: I give all glory to God because as I write this book, I recently retired after completing twenty years of active duty military service.)*

I told my chain of command, nurse case manager, and medical providers of my decision to stay on active duty, and we all partnered together in moving toward that objective. Everyone talked with me about the realities of my medical condition and the possibility that my career could soon end. They wanted me to succeed in returning to active-duty, but they also told me the harsh facts saying, "We hope your voice returns, but there are no guarantees. The damage to your right brachial plexus has caused paralysis to your right arm, and we don't know whether you will ever have the use of your right arm again." To stay on active duty, I definitely needed my voice; however, regarding my arm, current technological advances are allowing soldiers to return to active duty with prosthetics or limited use of limbs.

Physical Rehab

It was time to start my physical rehabilitation. Thankfully the Center for the Intrepid (CFI) is located on the SAMMC campus. The CFI is one of the Department of the Defenses premier rehabilitation centers.

Miracles happen daily at the facility, which is part of the reason I believe I was sent there. I needed a miracle, but frankly, I was afraid to start therapy. While in the hospital, people frequently asked me where was I being sent for rehabilitation, and I told them CFI. Almost everyone knew about their reputation, and they told me, "I have heard they are a great rehab center, but are very tough and will push you hard!" Considering my weakened physical condition, I was a little intimidated by what I was being told.

I started my rehab journey with occupational therapy. When most people think of rehabilitation centers, physical therapy generally comes to mind. Because the shooter's bullet severely damaged my nerve receptors, I had no use of my right arm and shoulder, and my muscles were rapidly weakening. So there was no need for physical therapy. My first therapist Katie, whom I believe is an angel in disguise, created my initial treatment plan. She devised a plan which included keeping my arm mobile by stretching it and focusing on activities of daily living with the use of only one arm. Katie's goal for me was to see that I could brush my teeth, take a shower, use the restroom, get dressed and undressed, etc. One of our early victories was when she taught me how to tie my shoe with one hand. It's been five years since the shooting, and I have yet to move up to physical therapy.

I spent my first year under Katie's care. Then my case was transferred to Melissa or "Mel" as I called her. For three years, Melissa was my occupational therapist. She built upon what Katie started. We tried all sorts of contraptions to get more use out of my right arm. She even tried attaching a different mechanical prosthesis to it, but they were too heavy.

Melissa was always willing to challenge her patients or keep them motivated. So, in November 2015, I said to her, "Next month, let's run the 13.1 mile Rock-n-Roll half marathon located in downtown San Antonio." As a Green Beret, I needed to keep the objective in sight, and to prevent becoming stagnate, I had to keep challenging myself. Luckily, I had a rock star therapist who was up to the task. We ran the 2015 Rock-n-Roll half marathon, and she beat me! *Shh! Don't tell anyone that I was beaten by my female therapist.*

Angel cheered us on from the starting line, and then she was at the finish line as the race ended. Running that race changed something inside me. I realized there was no disability which could stop me! The only thing that could prevent me from succeeding after my near-death experience was me. Katie and Melissa showed me that I might have limitations with my right arm movement, but it no longer defined my future. Now I was more than a mass shooting victim and survivor, I was a conqueror, and with Christ who strengthens me, I could do all things. Praise the Lord!

Early in my recovery, the routine was for Mason and me to wake up in the morning, eat breakfast, attend the accountability formation then go to the various medical appointments, which usually filled most of our day. Each Monday, I met with my nurse case manager, who organized my appointments for the week and scheduled any specialty appointments I needed. Her job was to make sure I had everything I needed for my recovery and that I was going to my scheduled appointments. She went "above and beyond the call of duty" for me. Nurse case managers generally manage only your medical care, but not mine. She took over my life, which was exactly what I needed at that time. Being a tough self-reliant former Green Beret, I didn't know how to ask for help. So, God put Cher in my life, and I can honestly say that I believe she also was divinely appointed as my case manager.

One day at an appointment at the CFI, something scary happened to me. I was working with my occupational therapist vigorously exercising my right arm when suddenly the neck strap for my throat trach came loose, and we heard the sound of oxygen rushing through the tube. The plastic tracheostomy tube slipped out of my neck, exposing the gaping hole. I was startled, not really knowing what to do next. I remember trying not to move while Katie calmly reached over and put the trach back in its place, secured the strap around my neck, then quickly went and found Dr. Marin to make sure I was okay. He walked up, checked it out, and said, "Everything is fine. You have nothing to worry about." Because of the severity of the damage to my neck and throat area, and the scarring, no one was taking chances. Understanding that my wounds were still healing, I got very nervous if I felt something wasn't normal.

Words cannot express my gratitude about the care I received from the staff at the CFI; they have become my family. If you've ever been a patient at a rehabilitation center, then you understand what I'm saying. A military facility adds an extra measure of camaraderie. When I was at the CFI, I felt safe. Early in my treatment, I asked the doctors how long I would need the tracheostomy in my throat, and was told to anticipate a minimum of six months. I think they were uncertain if it was going to be temporary or permanent. Thankfully, Jesus is the Great Healer because it was removed in two months!

On July 4th weekend 2014, after my tracheostomy had been removed earlier that week, I decided it would be good for Mason and me to head home for the Independence Day weekend and help Angel prepare our household items for the permanent move to San Antonio. While in Killeen, Angel and I decided to go to the movies. I was careful about what I was eating since it had not been very long since I was released to eat solid foods. But in the theater, I decided to eat popcorn. I mean, who goes to the movies and doesn't eat popcorn? Everything seemed to be fine until suddenly, I started coughing. I'm not sure what happened, but eventually, I began to cough up blood. It was not a lot of blood, but it was enough to scare me. Captain Cheatwood and his wife had joined us that evening. I remember getting the taste of blood in my mouth, my eyes got big, and my heart started pounding,

I looked at Angel and whispered, "I'm bleeding." It happened so fast I think I was simultaneously getting out of my seat to leave as I leaned over to Angel and told her; we needed to go to the hospital emergency room. Angel leaned over to the Cheatwood's and said, "I'm taking John to the hospital. He's bleeding." Captain Cheatwood followed us out of the movie theater. We quickly explained to him what had happened as we rapidly walked to the exit doors.

We checked into the emergency department at Darnall Medical Center on Fort Hood. We told the triage team that I was one of the survivors of the mass shooting, and I was bleeding from the location of the bullet wound. It did not take long for the staff to get me back to the examining room. Word must have gotten around that one of the victims from the shooting was in bed #2. Suddenly, approximately eight doctors and nurses walked into my room, just staring at me. Several began to ask if I remembered them. Apologizing, I told them that I didn't remember much of what happened once I arrived at the hospital on April 2, 2014. I clearly remember one of the doctors asking me, as he motioned for another doctor to come forward, "Do you remember this doctor?" "No," I answered. He replied, "This is the doctor that likely saved your life, he was the one that intubated you."

The doctor told me that if the curved plastic airway tube did not go into my neck at that moment, there was a high possibility they would have been unable to get one in at all because my throat was swelling so fast. That trip to the ER was a humbling moment for the doctors and me. The last time they saw me, my life was slipping away, and the chances of me pulling through were extremely low. But here I was three months after the incident, and I walked into the ER. The truth was that everyone believed they had witnessed a miracle, and God had used these doctors to assist with His handiwork!

The reason why I went to the ER from the movie theater turned out to be pretty minor. Since I had recently had my tracheotomy tube taken out, the whole site was pretty raw, so when I began coughing, it caused some minor bleeding. Because of the severity of my wound, the ER department called in the ENT surgeon that had initially worked on me, April 2, 2014. I felt good knowing the doctor who was going to examine me had knowledge of my injury, and it turned out to be another sobering reunion. As I write this book, it has been five years since that catastrophic date, and I am still meeting people who approach me and explain how they were in the ER when I was rushed in or put their fingers in my neck to stop the bleeding as I was being rushed to the operating room. I'm sure those I don't meet in this lifetime, I will see in Heaven, and I believe their halo will shine a little brighter for what they did for my fellow service members and me on April 2, 2014.

Rock-n-Roll Marathon With Melissa

Captain Arroyo & Angel

John & Angel Smiling After So Much Suffering

John Declares Victory At Shooting Site

John as Aide-de-Camp To MG Jones

Katie Watches John Strengthening Arm

Regaining the Use of My Right Arm

Motorcycle Before Accident

†††

CHAPTER EIGHT

My Life Transformed

As I continued in my recovery, I began sharing my story with anyone willing to listen. For nearly two and a half years, I wore a sling to support my right arm. It seemed to be a conversation starter, which usually led to me sharing how Jesus saved my life; however, I never pushed my beliefs on anyone. I simply shared what Jesus did for me that fateful day. Sometimes the person I was talking to would ask me to pray that Jesus would do the same for them. When you have the Creator of heaven and earth audibly speak to you and save you from a wound that usually killed instantly, you too would shout His name to the entire world at the loudest volume!

When people hear that I am a survivor of the second Fort Hood shooting, they generally are astounded. We see many tragic events unfolding on the news these days, but we rarely come across the victims or someone who is directly impacted. Then when they make the mental connection between what they saw on the news and me standing before them, it can be very emotional and shocking.

A common question people asked about my injury when they saw my sling was, "Did you have shoulder surgery?" My usual reply was, "No, I was shot at Fort Hood." That response generally caught people off guard. As I look back, that wasn't always the best response, but I had never been shot before, so responding differently was something I had to work on. I suppose no one can fault me for telling the truth, but I could have answered differently and made the situation a little less awkward.

Frequently, I have been asked, "Have you always been a believer in Jesus, or did the shooting lead you to Him?" Usually, I tell them I grew up knowing who Jesus was, and I went to Catholic Mass and church on Christmas and Easter, but that's because it was expected of me. However, I didn't have a real relationship with Jesus. I don't know how best to explain it, but I've always believed in Him. However, like most people, I lived by my own set of rules and standards. He was my God when it was convenient for me, especially when I joined the Army. Everyone has heard the expression "Foxhole prayers" when confronted with a difficult situation or even facing death, and that generally was my attitude early on as I grew in my faith.

I remember driving through the villages in Afghanistan, looking at all the ragged kids who chased our vehicles yelling at us to toss out candy, water, or food. I found myself praying for them and asking God to bless everyone I saw. After joining the U.S. Army and marrying Angel, I occasionally took my family to a church service because I knew I was supposed to do that based upon what I remembered from my childhood, but I left the church sanctuary as lost as when I walked in.

In 2009, three years before I was shot, my life was spiraling out of control because of my excessive use of alcohol. Sadly, my wife was along for this journey. We finally hit rock bottom, and that's when I had my "Come to Jesus moment." He asked, *Are you done?* He was calling Angel and me into a personal relationship with Him. I didn't know how to get there, so I did what most people do, I looked for worldly answers. We started marriage counseling, but it wasn't working because I was manipulating the counselor to be on my side in opposition to my loving wife. Then one Sunday, Jesus put it on my heart to walk into Rockfish Church. There I made the decision to change my life! When I walked through the doors somehow, I just knew I was supposed to be there. God wanted Angel and me to start counseling again, but this time it was spiritual counseling that was going to heal us. I'm not telling you that I've been perfect since the day I walked into the church. But I've gradually gotten better from who I once was, and today I don't serve Jesus because that's what my heritage tells me I should do. I serve because I now have a personal and close relationship with my Lord and Savior!

After being shot, many people who know me from my past probably thought, "He's just getting paid back for all the bad things he has done." I once had somebody tell me, "You must have done something evil in your past for that to happen to you." I agree with some of that, I didn't deserve the grace and mercy that was extended to me. Jesus could easily have told me, *You were a gang member, drug addict, liar, cheat, and thief.* But He didn't! Instead, He said, *"John, get up! You will not die. Today, I have commissioned you into my Army, now go and tell the world about me! I did not save you for you, you're just not that cool, and I did not save you for Me, or you would now be with Me in Heaven. I saved you for the people of this world who need to know I am real! Many people don't believe that I perform miracles anymore, which is why I am using you as living proof and evidence that I am always here for anyone who needs Me.*

What Are You Doing?

As my daily routine began to return to normal, I started attending church regularly. My friend Victor grew up in San Antonio, TX, and he and his family have been attending the same church for over twenty-five years. I attended their church when I first visited San Antonio while attending the Basic Officer Leaders Course. After the attack, Angel and I again began attending Bethesda Christian Church with Victor and his family. We were comfortable there. I felt safe with them, and they supported us in many ways.

After a few weeks of attending church on Sunday's and Wednesday's, I had this overwhelming feeling of needing to do more outside the church. I didn't understand what this new feeling was all about. The best way to explain it is; I didn't have peace with going to church on Sunday's then grabbing lunch and going home, and doing the same for Wednesdays. I loved Bethesda Church; the struggle was not with anyone else, but it was within me. I began to pray and ask Jesus, "Why am I feeling this way?" Then He began to speak to me. He said, *"John, what are you doing?"* I didn't understand at first, "What am I doing?" I was new to spiritually understanding when He's speaking. So, I replied, "Jesus, I don't understand your question, I'm recovering after being shot, I go to my doctor's appointments, and I go to church." He said, *"I didn't save you just so that you could go to church! I saved you to tell the world about me. You are living proof that my ways have not changed. I am still the Creator of miracles. Now go tell my people that I want to do the same for them!"* It wasn't long after this encounter with Jesus that I began to do more outside the confines of the church, and He started opening doors that no man could open.

Dr. Marin Helps John Reconfirm His Oath

Angel & John, Jr.

Soldier Who Saved Me Pins on Captain's Bars

John and Captain Cheatwood

MG Keenan Pins on Soldier's Medal

✝✝✝

CHAPTER NINE

Life After Near Death

In February 2015, I received an email from Colonel Eric Edwards, who was the former battalion commander of Fort Sam Houston's Warrior Transition Battalion, also known as the WTB. He asked me if I was interested in becoming the aide-de-camp for Major General Stephen Jones, who was the U.S. Army's Medical Department Center & School's commanding general. Colonel Edwards was the chief of staff for him. I turned down the job opportunity because, at the time, I thought, "There is no way that a young punk and former gangbanger who never completed anything until graduating from college after entering the Army would be qualified to be the aide to a major general. Besides that, I am a "knuckle-dragging" Green Beret, who has no filter from my brain to my mouth."

Then Colonel Edwards said, "The general has been involved with wounded warrior programs at Walter Reed Hospital in Bethesda, Maryland, and understands young soldiers who have been severely injured. He was commissioned through ROTC and placed in the reserves while in medical school then entered the military as a cardiologist. He performed his first duties as a primary care provider but ended his patient care to take on increasing roles of leadership. His last patient was Iraq's infamous leader, Saddam Hussein. He rose through the ranks, eventually commanding the Army's premier Medical Department Center & School, Health Readiness Center of Excellence (HRCOE). I think you can do the job. His aide is leaving in May, and the general is retiring in August. So, you will be his aide for the interim time and basically walk him out the door of his military career." At the end of the conversation, I declined his offer again even after learning that Colonel Edwards had served with the 7th Special Forces Group on deployment and that Major General Jones was a Ranger.

I had been at the Warrior Transition Battalion for approximately a year and was involved in working with the Center for the Intrepid, where they took us on different "field trips" to strengthen us in dealing with our disabilities. The excursions served two purposes for the service members. First, it was an opportunity to learn how to overcome our fears because of physical limitations; secondly, the trips got us out among the civilian private sector, which most wounded servicemen and women typically avoided.

From my counselors and therapist, I learned that I was reaching the end of my time with the WTB and was going to be transferred elsewhere, either back on active duty or through separation from the military as a civilian who was medically retired.

Two weeks after my conversation with Colonel Edwards, I received another email from him imploring me to reconsider my turn down to be the major general's aide-de-camp. At the time, I was assigned to the medical logistics section of Brooke Army Medical Center (BAMC) and decided to talk to my commanding officer Colonel Webb about accepting the job. He said, "John if you take this job, your career path will probably take a different trajectory than other second lieutenants. This opportunity will significantly enhance your career, and by not taking it, you will probably burn some bridges that you will ultimately regret. Besides, there is an application process that you have to undergo before you are approved for the job, so go ahead and see what happens next."

Responding back to Colonel Edward's email, I told him that I would like to apply for the job. He was pleased that I had agreed, and a few weeks later, I was appointed the aide-de-camp for Major General Stephen Jones. With my arm still in a sling and unable to use my right hand, I arrived at his office to do a "route recon" i.e., check the situation out. I met with his current aide who briefed me on some of the required duties I was expected to perform. Then I met with the executive officer who was a lieutenant colonel and asked him, "Sir, how did I get this job? There likely are ten highly-trained West Point graduates who are better qualified for this position that I am; a hard-charging Green Beret from the streets of Southern California who only has the use of his left arm and hand." Smiling at me from across his desk, he said, "John, this job was never going to anyone other than you." Sitting in his office, I knew this was a God-inspired opportunity to give me a platform to share my story of strength, hope, and recovery to the world. I also knew that I was going to improve my communication skills with people of higher rank and civilian status and how to operate strategically and more effectively than ever before. Shortly after I began my new job, Major General Jones decided to delay his retirement for one year.

From May 2015 to August 2016, I was the aide to the highest-ranking medical doctor in the U.S. Army. I was responsible for coordinating all of his travel arrangements and scheduling of events in the United States. Very quickly, I learned never to make a mistake, or it would be my last one as his aide; and I also learned the meaning of "servitude." In my official capacity, my sole purpose was to make his life better, more comfortable, and more effective in carrying out his duties as head of the medical branch for the United States Army. For fifteen months, I performed well in my position as Major General

Jones's aide-de-camp and received a certificate of meritorious service from him when he retired.

Then, I was assigned to the Basic Officer Leader Course, which was under the command of the U.S. Army Medical Department Center & School. That was where all incoming doctors, dentists, physician assistants, and medical personnel first entered the U.S. Army. After leaving the general's aide assignment, I stayed under the same command and at the same post and with that unit at Fort Sam Houston, Texas, from August 2016 until my retirement in November 2018.

700 Club TV Video

A few months after my shooting at Fort Hood, I began having frequent conversations with God about how he was going to use that event and me to help others in crisis. One afternoon I was sitting in my living room watching the Christian Broadcasting Network's (CBN) "700 Club" program when the announcer said, "If any of you have a testimony and would like to share it with our audience, send it to us." I thought, *"God, am I getting a prompting from you to tell my story to others?"* Sitting there for a few minutes, I decided to type up a rough draft of the incident and email it to the address shown on the TV screen. After several weeks of not receiving a response to my email, I forgot about it.

Approximately one year later, my telephone rang, and a 700 Club producer asked me if I was 1ˢᵗ Lieutenant John Arroyo. He explained that my email had been misplaced and had been sitting on someone's desk for almost a year, and they would very much like to do a video interview with Angel and me about my near-death encounter. I truly believe that the producer's call was providentially delayed to allow my voice box and wounds to recover sufficiently that I could then tell my story in a compelling and "soul-saving" way.

After exhaustive vetting of my story, the show's primary producer called me and said, "John we would really like to make a video of your story and run it on the 700 Club program, but we would like to shoot it from your wife Angel's point of view and call it; *Military wife hopes for the impossible after shooting.*" Thrilled at the offer, I immediately gave permission to begin the process.

The video was professionally prepared and shot on location at Fort Sam Houston, Texas. The 700 Club crew, producers, and staff were great to work with and were very supportive of Angel and me during the filming process. In fact, I still use the video clip in many of my presentations at churches, schools, and military installations where I speak. After viewing it, the audience's reaction usually is one of "shock and awe" to use a well-known military cliché. I'm very grateful to the 700 Club and the Christian Broadcasting Network (CBN) for spending the time, effort, and money to produce a high-quality video that has substantially helped my personal ministry at speaking engagements.

Jeff Wells Acknowledgment

A close personal friend of mine, Jeff Wells, is a realtor in San Antonio. We met while I was undergoing rehab at Fort Sam Houston's Center for the Intrepid, and his organization (with the help of SWBC mortgage) purchased a recumbent bicycle for me to use in my therapy. Jeff is a former U.S. Army captain who was stationed at Fort Hood, then left the military and with his wife Kristen, started Wells Property Group in San Antonio, Texas. His support and encouragement, soon after I was shot, has been instrumental in my overall recovery, and today I know that if ever I need anything I can call Jeff and he will be there for my family and me.

In 2010 Jeff incorporated a 501(c) 3 organization called Wish for Our Heroes. It assists military families struggling with financial burdens caused by frequent deployments, TDY family separations, and the daily strains of military life. By providing 100% transparency for all donations, and a unique focus on assisting military members not covered by other charities, Wish for Our Heroes assists families by providing basic needs and building family cohesiveness before, during, and after deployments.

He started the non-profit organization in memory of his father, 1SG Thomas G. Wells (1933-2009), a Marine Corps veteran of the Korean and Vietnam wars, as well as all active-duty military heroes.

Meeting Dave Roever

While attending a church service in Seguin, Texas, it was announced that Dave Roever was going to be the guest speaker for their "wild game" dinner that evening. I asked the pastor who Dave Roever was, and he replied, "He's a Vietnam veteran who goes around sharing his story about being burned alive by a white phosphorus grenade in 1969 while he was part of a brown water, black beret, special naval warfare unit, patrolling the rivers and transporting Navy SEALs." I said, "I've never heard of him before but would like to attend the meeting."

Later that afternoon, Dave arrived at the gymnasium, and the pastor introduced me to him and said, "Dave, this is John Arroyo, who was one of the shooting victims at Fort Hood in April 2014." Shaking my hand, Dave replied, "I'm so sorry, lieutenant. That was a tragic event and should never have happened. Here's my card let's stay in contact and maybe I will see you at one of my speaking events or at my ranch in South Texas or in Colorado where we take active-duty military and veterans. We have a program called Winning with Integrity, and it helps anyone suffering from PTSD. We have a couples' program and a woman's only group, and we bring them in and work with them as they deal with the impact of their trauma." I said, "Dave, my wife and I would really love to be involved with your organization in some capacity." Then as if he did not hear me, he continued setting out his books, which he intended to sell at the event and other merchandise related to his ministry.

Angel and I took our seats in the gymnasium, and about ten minutes into Dave's presentation, he stopped, looked at me, and said, "Lieutenant, stand up!" Looking around to see if there were any other lieutenants present, I realized that he was speaking to me, so I reluctantly stood up. Dave raised his left hand and with his only functioning index finger pointed at me and said, "John, you and I are going to work together someday, so stay in contact with me. This is a divine appointment, and we are supposed to partner together and minister to anyone who has suffered a traumatic injury or event."

The next Monday, I was anxiously awaiting a phone call from Dave, thinking I'm going to be traveling around with him telling my story to churches and organizations like he does. In the presenting of his story, he has the audience laughing one minute and crying the next. I thought, *"I want to be able to do the same thing when I tell my story."*

But for the next four years, I never heard from Dave Roever. Then in October 2017, several buddies of mine and I attended one of Dave's "Winning with Integrity" sessions at his Junction, Texas ranch. While there, in a conversation with Dave, I told him that a newspaper article written by BAMC Public Affairs was about me being shot at Ft. Hood and included the story of his friend Katie Blanchard. Katie was a burn victim who, while serving as a nurse at Fort Leavenworth, had been deliberately set on fire at her work. The article was about workplace violence. He said, "I read the article and liked it, so tomorrow when we are at the lake I'd like to visit with you for a few minutes. I can't stay out in the sun very long because it hurts my burn scars too badly, but I do want to talk with you."

The next day, after waiting my turn, I finally sat down with Dave, and he said, "John can you come up to Fort Worth and meet with my staff and me so that I can show you what our complete operation is all about and how the apprenticeship program fits into our organization?" Surprised by the request, I said, "Yes sir! I would like that very much." So, in December 2017, a friend of mine, Shade Bounds, and I began to drive to Fort Worth. However, the evening before, a major ice storm covered Interstate 35 north of San Antonio to Austin with black ice.

Tightly gripping the steering wheel, I slowly drove along, and then I turned to my friend and said, "Dave will understand if we can't make it because of the weather, so I think we need to turn around." My friend said, "John, this is really important, so let's keep on going and just take it easy." Thinking, *"This is like having Jesus and the Holy Spirit sitting next to me, urging me to continue on."* North of Austin, a couple of hours later, the sun came out, and there was no ice on the highway, so we drove to Fort Worth with no difficulty.

I met Pastor Dan Dang, an ordained minister and Vietnamese refugee, Al Roever, and Dave Wallace. I was amazed at the worldwide ministry and the impact it had on hundreds of thousands of people around the globe since Dave's injury in 1969. After a couple of hours, he said to me, "John, I would like to offer you the opportunity to come work for us at this organization. You can do so as an employee or as a steppingstone to launch your own ministry. So, discuss this with your wife Angel and see if that's something you both want to do, but I want to make this very clear to you. Don't come here with the expectation of making lots of money. This work is about souls! We are not here to make people millionaires, but we will make them rich in The Kingdom."

On the way back to San Antonio, I was fervently praying that Dave would allow me to work from my home because I was sure that Angel was not going to be in favor of us moving to Fort Worth. Arriving at my house, we sat down, and I explained to her that Dave offered me a job that required us to move there. Looking at me for a moment, Angel finally said, "Yes! I think that's what we are supposed to do. That's what we're called to do." I was flabbergasted by her response and thrilled at this new chapter that was about to begin in our life. That night she had a dream in which she gave birth to two babies; one an infant and the other a toddler, and I believe that dream was God's way of confirming this "divine appointment" as an opportunity to begin a new stage in our life.

The next morning I sent an email to Dave telling him that I would like to go to work for him, but it was going to be about a year before I retired from active duty. Emotionally, the next year was probably the hardest time of my life with all of the "doubts" and "fears" and "what if's" that ran through my head. I thought, *How can a young punk, gangbanger from Southern California with no Bible background, and is a U.S. Army Green Beret expect to work with a man like Dave Roever who traveled for nine years with Billy Graham on his crusades?"* Then God said to me, *"John, don't worry, everything will be revealed to you as you need to understand it."*

In late 2018, I retired from the U.S. Army, and Angel, and I moved to Fort Worth, where we both began to work for Dave's organization in the Roever Educational Assistance Program (REAP). There are four other programs that he also operates. The first is Roever Evangelistic Association, where Dave speaks at churches and faith-based conferences. Then there is REAP International, working in approximately thirty-five nations, teaching an estimated one hundred and twenty thousand students.

There also is the Roever Foundation, which works with the United States Department of Defense (DOD), where Dave speaks to the active-duty military about resiliency and overcoming seemingly impossible situations. He also speaks at schools, business conferences, and civic organizations. Finally, there is Reap International Bible College, which is affiliated with the School of Urban Missions (SUM). Through them, I am currently working on my Master's Degree in Christian Leadership *(with a 4.0 GPA!)*.

Sometimes I don't think I'm qualified to do this work, but then I remember God doesn't bring the "qualified" into the fold. What he does is "qualifies" those who are "called" and this retired Special Forces operator is definitely called to this work and this ministry. The motto of the Green Berets is "De Oppresso Liber," which means "Free the Oppressed." Isaiah 58:6 says ... *to let the oppressed go free.* In Luke 4:18, Jesus says we are ... *to* set at liberty those who are oppressed. Both verses represent my heart's desire to set people free from their sins, strongholds, and spiritual oppressors.

I believe the spirit of the Lord was upon me when he anointed me to preach the gospel to the nations. The day I donned the Green Beret uniform was also the day I put on the armor of God and was commissioned into His Army. Isaac Newton once said, "If I have seen further than others, it is by standing upon the shoulders of giants." Being mentored by Dave Roever, who was mentored by Billy Graham, both mighty men of God, places me at a higher level of understanding than I could possibly have achieved on my own. Their passion for the gospel ignites and inflames me today, and I am "all in" for preaching the gospel and expanding the kingdom.

Life After Near Death

John & His Mentor Dave Roever

God's Warrior

New Life; New Focus

✝✝✝

Hope Restored

We've come to the end of the telling of our story up to this point in our lives. We are happy that you took this journey with us and we do hope that you enjoyed it. However, we didn't write this book so you could read a good story with all its highs and lows and then move on to another telling of a different story. No, this book is a framework of restoration and redemption. As we have prayed over the development and publication of this book, we also have prayed for you. We have prayed your reading through the pages will reveal the endless love Christ has for you in a heart-moving way. God's word written in Ecclesiastes tells us that He placed eternity into the hearts of mankind, and it is the deepest longing anyone ever has. Our story was written down and sent forth to stir and awaken your God-given desire for eternity and in so doing, to point the way for you to enter into your eternal life today.

By telling our story and the miracles we have experienced, we want to help you see what Jesus can do. He healed my body when all the experts and capable physicians said it wouldn't happen. I have lived out His promise found in Romans 8:11, *The Spirit of God, who raised Jesus from the dead, lives in you. And just as God raised Christ Jesus from the dead, he will give life to your mortal bodies by this same Spirit living within you.*

He protected me from certain death when I came face to face with the shooter by making me invisible before his eyes. His word tells us how He did that in Psalm 27, *One thing I ask from the LORD, this only do I seek: that I may dwell in the house of the LORD all the days of my life, to gaze on the beauty of the LORD and to seek him in his temple. For in the day of trouble, he will keep me safe in his dwelling; he will hide me in the shelter of his sacred tent and set me high upon a rock.* God is so good, that the moment I cried out for Him, he hid me in His presence and saved my life.

He healed our family and restored our relationships. Chapter 3 of Ephesians records Paul's prayer in which he says, *"For this reason, I kneel before the Father, from whom every family in heaven and on earth derives its name."* He created families and created all of us to be in a relationship with each other. When we gave our hearts to Him, of course, He wanted to heal our family and restore it to the way He planned it - filled with love!

He made a path out of the wilderness of lost purpose for us when we were unable to find a way to this new life. He has lifted us up out of the empty way we lived our lives and has filled our days with abundance and joy. Truly, we have experienced what is written in 1 Corinthians 2:9, *"The Holy Writings say, 'No eye has ever seen or no ear has ever heard or no mind has ever thought of the wonderful things God has made ready for those who love Him.'"*

He can make all things new, just as He said He can, and we know this because we have experienced the newness. Our faith has become new-found sight as He has done wonder upon wonder in our lives. We have prayed that you will come to believe in the power of Jesus through the telling of this story.

Can you relate to what Angel and I went through? Not necessarily being attacked, shot, and coming close to dying. But have you been so broken by your personal experiences all the hope you had was destroyed? Have there been times you felt you were surrounded by a darkness that you could feel and touch; darkness so complete you thought you would never see a bright ray of hope again?

Frequently, an empty existence without Jesus in it is referred to as "life." However, life like that is filled with brokenness, struggles, and emptiness that can't be filled. No matter what your situation is, Jesus can come into the circumstances and restore real life for you. I know that is true because He has done that for Angel and me! I hope now, you can believe it too. But do you believe He **_will_** do that for you? Your belief that Jesus can do mighty things may be strong, but do you have Faith that He loves you and wants to bring good into **_your_** life?

When Jesus was walking on earth, his disciples were following Him and seeing Him do many miracles. Then came a time when He sent them out to minister to others to do what they had seen Him do. The Book of Matthew's 17th chapter records that at first, they struggled and didn't see the same results, so they asked Jesus, "Why can't we do what You did?" He told them they didn't have faith. They knew He *"could"* because they had seen him do miracle after miracle. But they didn't have faith that He *"would"* change them so they would live a life like He wanted to give them. Perhaps that's how you feel. I hope you can hear the good news Jesus told His disciples; *"All you need is faith the size of a tiny mustard seed!"*

If you believe Jesus truly is the Savior, Redeemer, and Prince of Peace, are you ready to open up to a relationship with Him? Are you ready to let Him take that tiny seed of faith you have that maybe, just maybe, He really does want to live in your heart? If you do, He will show you what it is He wants to do in your life. As He does that, your faith will grow. He already knows about all your bad days, bad results, bad thoughts, and He wants to give you days filled with wonder, good results exceedingly more than you can think or imagine, and He wants His thoughts to become your thoughts.

The first step to experiencing real life with Jesus begins with doing what He told me to do. ***Get up! Get up*** out of the past, out of the brokenness, out of the labels, lies, and limitations you believe about who you are. ***Get up*** out of the darkness that is bringing death to you and to all your hopes and dreams and come stand in the glorious light of the love of God.

The writer of the book of Hebrews tells us that for the *"Joy"* that was set before Him, Jesus chose the cross. What joy came to Jesus through that horrible time of crucifixion? The joy of having you choose to have faith in Him. He took every bit of the darkness in your life caused by the sin you have committed and the pain from the sin others committed toward you into defeat as He died on the cross. He did that so you could have faith in Him. He has the joy that is His because He knows that when you choose Him, He can be with you in a close and amazing relationship that will strengthen, restore, and redeem you from all that might come your way this side of heaven. His greatest joy of all, however, is knowing you will be with Him for all eternity.

Jeremiah 29:11 is a widely known Scripture that is frequently quoted and printed on almost everything; walls, bumpers, mugs, and tee shirts. It is a beautiful and powerful promise from our Living God as it assures us, *"For I know the plans I have for you,"* declares the LORD, *"plans to prosper you and not to harm you, plans to give you hope and a future."* He was speaking to His children, whose rebellion and stubbornness led them into captivity for seventy years. They were in a shattered place with no hope, so God sent His word to them. My world was instantly shattered, and that same word was true for me. It is important to notice the words that follow in the next two verses: *"Then you will call upon Me and go and pray to Me, and I will listen to you. And you will seek Me and find Me, when you search for Me with all your heart.*" He knew His children would one day call out to Him, so He made plans for them when they came back to Him.

In the darkest, most shattered moment of my life, all I could say was part of His name; but He heard, and His response was to open the door to an incredible life for Angel and me. What fantastic plan might Jesus have for you, just waiting until you call out for Him to come live in your heart? To have our hope restored, we need only to **_Get Up_** and seek Him with our whole heart. Once we get up, then we have to look up. Looking up to Him and fixing our eyes on Him will lead us to let go of all the bitterness and darkness stored in our hearts. Then we can seek Him and Him alone and find the only source of real hope there is. That is how you will discover the plan He made for you.

Maybe some of what you have been through seems completely senseless. I felt that way. How could I have gone through intense combat in a war-torn foreign country, then return safely to my homeland only to experience a brutal, life-threatening attack on an American military fort? It seemed senseless then, and it is impossible to really make sense of it today. However, it wasn't purposeless. God didn't cause this to happen, but God had a plan to bring purpose out of the senseless. He has a plan and a purpose for you, as well. When God redeems your life, He will use your story to touch others in a way that only you can. You, too, will be able to comfort others with the same comfort you have been given by *"The God of all comfort"* as promised in 2 Corinthians 1:4 *"…who comforts us in all our troubles so that we can comfort those in any trouble with the comfort we ourselves receive from God."*

God told me to "Get up!" and I have reflected on that a great deal. In the first chapter of Jeremiah, the Bible records another time when He told someone to get up. When He was preparing Jeremiah to take His important message out into the world, He said, *"Get up and prepare for action. Go out and tell them everything I tell you to say."* I was told to get up so my wife wouldn't die. God knew I loved Angel so much that I would get up for her, even if I didn't have the strength to do it for myself. That represents the kind of love God has for all His children. He is telling Jeremiah to get up so His children wouldn't die. As Angel and I have seen the difference having Him in our lives has made, and He has connected us to so many people, He has given us a strong desire to go out and tell them everything He has told us to say! Do you have someone in your life who you love enough that now you, too, will get up and look up to Jesus?

Get up! Look up! Then we are called to "Reach up!" We are to stretch to follow Jesus and His higher, life-giving ways. Every day is a new adventure for Angel and me as we let Him lead us wherever He needs us to proclaim His Good News. There is no way the two of us could have created or sustained this journey without the help of our Lord and Savior, Jesus Christ. There are days that bring challenges, and sometimes we can't see where we are going, and even other times when we don't understand what is happening. Those days are the very best since they remind us that He is so much greater than us, and is doing so much more than we ever could be and do without Him.

The love the Father has for us all, expressed by Jesus' life, death and resurrection, and sustained through the power of the Holy Spirit, is the only source of true hope that is lasting and real! Our loving Father and our Savior have been ever-present sustaining us with Holy Spirit power, wisdom and knowledge, and daily granting us grace. We pray you will give your old life to Him, let Him into your heart, and come join us in this marvelous light-filled journey as we seek more of Him.

Finally, I want to say that from an unspeakable tragedy, incredible good has resulted!

John M. Arroyo, Jr.

Hope Restored

Renewed Vows

Beauty For Ashes

Restored Family

††

ACKNOWLEDGEMENTS

Operation Warrior RECONnect
Wish For Our Heroes
Operation Finally Home
Fisher House
Sentinels of Freedom
Green Beret Foundation
Taskforce Dagger
Operation Comfort
Wounded Warrior Project
Semper Fi Fund
Homes Fit For Heroes
Disabled American Veterans
Operation Healing Forces
Freedom Alliance

Stan Corvin, Jr.

Born in 1945 in a small town in West Texas, Stan grew up in a military family. His father, a career United States Air Force fighter pilot from 1940 to 1974, retired as a colonel, and his mother was an elementary school teacher who frequently taught at many of the bases where they were stationed.

After attending Texas Tech University for his undergraduate studies, Stan was drafted into the U.S. Army. In basic training, he was accepted into the Army's helicopter flight school and graduated nine months later in December 1967. Serving in the U.S. Army from 1967 to 1974, he flew helicopters in Vietnam in 1968-69 as a "Loach" pilot for a "Hunter Killer" team and then as a covert operations pilot for the CIA in 1971-72 attaining the rank of captain. Stan resigned his commission in 1974 to pursue a career in banking.

In 1983, Stan was chosen to be the Executive Director of the Vietnam Veterans Leadership Program (VVLP), an advocacy initiative funded by the U.S. Action Agency and supported by President Ronald Reagan. Its purpose was to assist veterans suffering from PTSD and active-duty personnel transitioning out of the military into civilian life. Speaking at civic groups, churches, and schools, Stan's goal was to change the image of the Vietnam veteran from a "Rambo" style self-loathing individualist to a productive member of American society.

In 2014, after forty years in banking and commercial lending, Stan retired, and in 2015 wrote, and published the first edition of *Vietnam Saga: Exploits of a Combat Helicopter Pilot,* a vivid personal memoir about his three years of flying during the Vietnam War including his story of being shot down twice in ten minutes at Khe Sanh trying to save an American USAF F-4 fighter pilot who had bailed out and was surrounded by 12,500 NVA soldiers. Stan survived for thirteen hours laying in a muddy rice paddy after being shot four times in the chest and stomach by an enemy AK-47!

In 2015, Stan was asked by a close friend, Major General Carl G. Schneider, to write his memoirs about flying jets in Korea and Vietnam and how he rose through the ranks from an enlisted private to a two-star general in thirty years; a feat only a few men in the history of the United States military have ever accomplished. Thus *Jet Pioneer: A Fighter Pilot's Memoir* was written and published.

Then in 2017, Stan wrote and published the second edition of *Vietnam Saga: Exploits of a Combat Helicopter Pilot,* which included expanded text and photographs.

In February 2018, Stan published *Echoes of the Hunt,* which was the first place winner of the 2019 Texas Authors Association's Book Contest for hunting adventures. Taking place in West Texas, it is a true story of Stan's ten-day stalking of a trophy mule deer. While sitting alone beside a warm fireplace and in a cold deer stand, he also recalls childhood stories of hunting adventures with his father, grandfather, and uncles.

In September 2018, Stan co-authored and published *Vietnam Abyss: A Journal of Unmerited Grace.* It is the inspiring true story of

Michael J. Snook a Vietnam Veteran who descends into the darkness of chronic Post Traumatic Stress Disorder (PTSD), alcoholism, insanity and multiple confinements in a Veterans Administration psychiatric ward then later through his participation in PTSD counseling sessions and the program of Alcoholics Anonymous recovers and becomes a born-again Christian and an ordained minister.

All of the books are available through Amazon Books, Kindle, Barnes & Noble, and audiobooks on Audible.com and iTunes.

Stan lives with his wife near Nashville, Tennessee, and they have seven adult children and sixteen grandkids.

Stan Corvin, Jr.
Co-Author